MAKING YOUR YOUR FIRST YEAR A SUCCESS

SECOND EDITION

We dedicate this book to Louise and Louis.
They are patient, kind, and understanding.

MAKING YOUR FIRST YEAR A SUCCESS

A CLASSROOM SURVIVAL GUIDE
FOR
MIDDLE AND HIGH SCHOOL TEACHERS

SECOND EDITION

ROBERT L. WYATT III
J. ELAINE WHITE

CORWIN PRESS
A SAGE Publications Company
Thousand Oaks, CA 91320

For information:

Corwin Press
A Sage Publications Company
2455 Teller Road
Thousand Oaks, California 91320
www.corwinpress.com

Sage Publications Ltd.
1 Oliver's Yard
55 City Road
London EC1Y 1SP
United Kingdom

Sage Publications India Pvt. Ltd.
B-42, Panchsheel Enclave
Post Box 4109
New Delhi 110 017 India

373.11
. W93
2007

Printed in the United States of America.

Library of Congress Cataloging-in-Publication Data

Wyatt, Robert Lee, 1940-
Making your first year a success : a classroom survival guide for middle and high school teachers / Robert L. Wyatt III, J. Elaine White. — 2nd ed.
        p. cm.
Includes bibliographical references.
ISBN 978-1-4129-4956-9 (cloth) — ISBN 978-1-4129-4957-6 (pbk.)
    1. First year teachers—Handbooks, manuals, etc. 2. High school teachers—Handbooks, manuals, etc. 3. High school teaching—Handbooks, manuals, etc.
I. White, J. Elaine. II. Title.
LB2844.1.N4W93 2007
373.11—dc22

                    2006034108

This book is printed on acid-free paper.

07 08 09 10 11 10 09 08 07 06 05 04 03 02 01

Acquisitions Editor:	Rachel Livsey
Editorial Assistant:	Phyllis Cappello
Production Editor:	Sarah K. Quesenberry
Copy Editor:	Edward Meidenbauer
Typesetter:	C&M Digitals (P) Ltd.
Proofreader:	Caryne Brown
Cover Designer:	Michael Dubowe
Graphic Artist:	Lisa Riley

Contents

Acknowledgments

The contributions of the following reviewers are gratefully acknowledged.

Jane D. Adair
Resource Specialist
Long Beach Polytechnic High School
Long Beach Unified School District
Long Beach, California

Wendy Caszatt-Allen
Teacher
Mid-Prairie Middle School
Kalona, Iowa

Catherine Kilfoyle Duffy
English Department Chairperson
Three Village Central District
Stony Brook, New York

Catherine H. Payne
Principal
W. R. Farrington High School
Honolulu, Hawaii

About the Authors

Robert L. Wyatt, III, is Professor Emeritus of Education at East Central University in Ada, Oklahoma, where he has taught secondary pedagogy and methods classes for the past 16 years. He also teaches graduate courses such as philosophy of education, young adult literature, contemporary issues, techniques of research, curriculum development, supervision of instruction, and public relations for school administrators. He taught education courses as a graduate instructor at the University of Oklahoma while completing his doctorate. He has also taught courses in education and English at New Mexico State University and at three junior colleges in Texas. He has more than 25 years' experience teaching secondary and middle school in Texas, New Mexico, and Oklahoma. He has led more than 150 seminars and workshops for staff development in the past 16 years, and has twice received East Central University's Teacher Excellence award, which can only be awarded to the same person every 4 years and is nominated by students and elected by peer review.

Wyatt is a language arts specialist for elementary and secondary education. He teaches undergraduate courses in language arts methods, secondary social studies methods, portfolio construction, strategies of teaching (secondary), student teaching seminar and children's literature. He has authored *Tent Repertoire Theater: The History of the Haverstock Tent Show—The Show With a Million Friends,* published by Southern Illinois University Press in 1997, and, with Sandra Looper, *So You Have to Have a Portfolio: A Teacher's Guide to Preparation and Presentation,* published by Corwin Press, in second edition in 2004.

Wyatt is also a selling artist of watercolor and oil paintings, having done more than 150 paintings in the past few years. He is former President-Director of ACT II, Ada's Community Theater, which produces as many as 11 plays each year. He has directed more than thirty productions in each of the past 10 years. He has three novels out for publisher review, is a former owner-editor of a weekly newspaper (with Louise, his wife of 45 years), and has self-published three books of local Oklahoma history. He has a daughter, a son, a daughter-in-law, and a grand-dog.

J. Elaine White is Associate Professor of English at the University of Southern Mississippi and teaches at the Gulf Coast teaching site. In addition to maintaining teaching responsibilities, White serves as program coordinator for the Gulf Coast English faculty and directs the Live Oak Writing Project, an affiliate of the National Writing Project. Previous to teaching at the college level, she taught for 25 years in public schools. Her classroom experiences include teaching music for grades 1–12, directing choirs that received superior ratings at state vocal contests, coaching students in vocal solo and ensemble work, teaching English for grades 9–12, developing honors and advanced placement English programs, working with student writers who achieved state and national recognition, teaching GED courses, and serving as district-wide curriculum director. She is listed in *Who's Who Among America's Teachers*, an honor awarded through student nominations and peer review.

White is a secondary English education specialist. At The University of Oklahoma and The University of Southern Mississippi, she has taught undergraduate courses in reading-writing theory and application, language study for teachers, literature for adolescents, and secondary English methods. She has also taught graduate courses in young adult literature, teacher action research, and advanced methods in the teaching of English. She has made presentations at meetings of the National Council of Teachers of English, the Assembly for Expanded Perspectives on Learning, and the National Writing Project. Publications include articles for *ALAN Review, Voice* (a publication of National Writing Project), and writing lessons for software created by the American Educational Corporation.

When not involved in educational activities, White writes poetry, works with children's choirs, plays organ, paints, and spoils her grandchildren.

Introduction

B ecause both of us have had so many years of teaching experience, we thought we had some ideas that would help new teachers become effective, and even help those who had been around a while and needed to be rejuvenated. We had "been there, done that," and it just seemed to us that it would be great if some of the forgotten pedagogy that we had taught in our education classes could be revisited in a compact little guide book. We coupled practical experience with these emphases from pedagogical skills. Anyone reading the book would know that we cared. After all, we were teachers long before we were professors.

So much criticism has been leveled at public education and how it is not meeting the needs of students. Those who criticize surely must understand that education is an evolving profession. As we learn more about teaching and learning, our practice grows and changes. Sometimes the changes are good and will show immediate improvement. Sometimes they take time, and improvement comes slowly. Sometimes the things we try are not effective, and they have to be abandoned. We have sifted through many such items and have filled this book with what we feel are the most effective, useful pedagogical skills.

The purpose of this book is to share the most exciting things we could about teaching. We wanted to help anticipate some questions you would face as a new teacher and to give you practical advice for making the first years of teaching successful.

With that in mind, we began talking about our book and our ideas to our own students. They said that in our pedagogy and professional education classes we had been talking about authenticity and empowerment, and they thought that our book idea sounded real enough and practical enough to be authentic. They thought that having a guide such as our book would help empower them to be effective teachers. We liked their use of *authentic* and *empowerment*, two items on which we had spent so much time in class.

In multiple conversations with our students, one took the old Chinese proverb about teaching a man to fish and rephrased it as a statement about teaching. We had heard it many times over the years, but it still makes sense and is excellent material for making a middle school and secondary teacher effective. He wrote, "I want to teach because I have always heard that if you tell me, I will forget it; if you show me, I will remember; if you involve me, I will understand."

One of them compared a teacher to a savior,

> I want to be a part of education because I know that education can save the world. It won't make all of those we are about to teach geniuses, but we may change just one of their lives, and then that one may make such an impact that he or she will change the world.

One commented that teaching was

> not a profession that you can leave at your workplace. It is so enjoyable that you make it both your profession and your hobby. When you think of teaching as a hobby, then you go to school every day thinking what fun it is to spend the day playing at your hobby. I want to go to work to play every day!

Their comments stirred our souls, and that is why we wanted to make them a guidebook for being effective. We offer it to you. We hope you can find some ideas that will help our newfound "hobby" bring you all the joy it has brought us.

We have learned that every teacher must have a plan, a guideline to bring that goal into some semblance of being. We feel that this new edition can help teachers in creating a plan of getting off to a good start. Yes, there are other ways to achieve this goal, and those other ways can work, too, if one is willing to put heart and soul into the effort of making ideas work. We have just articulated some thoughts on what has worked for us over the years. We have enhanced some thoughts, upgraded some thoughts, and rethought some thoughts. We trust we still have an easy-to-follow roadmap for a successful beginning for you to become a good teacher. We want to keep you in the profession, and we want you to be happy in it.

In this new edition, we told a few more actual stories to illustrate our points. We tightened up any references to theory because we wanted the book to be theory based, but we still wanted it to be a practical approach, not just theoretical. We updated using our approach to meet the expectations of No Child Left Behind. We updated our chapter on technology even though technology changes so rapidly that no book can keep absolutely current with those challenges. We added differentiation in the classroom and in lesson planning. We connected better to curriculum standards issued by the district, the state, and the national organizations, and gave you some ideas of how to achieve them using our guide. We recognized the need for more rigorous discussion on handling classroom management, and we reacted to those needs.

There is no panacea, no pill to make everything work the way that we think it should. We wish that we could just give you an ironclad rule instead of your having to take some of what we have said in the book and apply it to your needs as they arise. We do know that if you follow our thoughts, you will not be a failure. You may not be the "teacher of the year" your first year in the field, but you could be. The book is designed to renew ideas for those who have been teaching some time and who may need some reminders of the importance of being revitalized in their zeal for their profession. All of us can become complacent, so a little boost of new energy cannot be harmful.

Whatever we have achieved, we just wish you the best in whichever capacity you use the book. Know that we have believed and practiced these applications over our careers, and we have felt success and joy in our profession.

CHAPTER ONE

Surviving in School

YOUR OWN CLASSROOM

E very teacher remembers the first day of "real" school, the day when you walk into your very own classroom—no university supervisor, no mentor teacher—just you and your students. It is a moment filled with both anticipation and apprehension. You have years of preparation for this time. You have spent hours reading, observing, writing lesson plans, and practicing your role and skills. And yet as you wait for your students, you are just a little nervous. What will you do when you are left alone with these people? How will you negotiate this first year? How will you implement the things you've studied and learned? Will you be able to manage students? Will you know what to do in dealing with students and parents? Will you find a friend and mentor on the faculty? What happens if you make mistakes? Although your experience is unique, it is also similar to the experience of every new teacher. No one has faced that first year absolutely certain of what to expect or of how to handle the challenges inherent in teaching.

There are so many aspects to "learning the ropes" that it is really an ongoing process. This is critical to remember. Teaching is a dynamic rather than static process, and even career teachers have to change procedures or approaches periodically. As you work through your first year of teaching, realize that this initial time is really on-the-job training. Even after all the methods classes and pedagogical training, there is no way to be 100% prepared for teaching. All of your college preparation has helped you get ready to teach your subject, but you won't actually learn all that's involved in the profession until you are in a room, all alone, with no one to call on for help. The first year will be focused not so much on what you teach as on your learning about how to teach and about how school really works. And even though you may wonder if you aren't more of a learner than a teacher at times during this first year, remember that you are involved in the process of learning to teach—a process that should last through your entire career.

One of the most important things to do during your first year of teaching is to be kind to yourself. Realize that it will take about 3 years for you to feel like you really know what you are doing. A former student called this week, excited about beginning her third year of teaching. "You were right!" she exclaimed. "This is my third year, and I really think I know what I'm doing. That first year was rough, but I didn't damage anyone," she chuckled. "Last year was better, but I still felt a little unsure. This year, however, I am ready to start. I think I have it figured out, but even better than that, I know I can do this."

LOOKING AT AND SETTING UP YOUR NEW ENVIRONMENT

Many schools provide campus tours for new teachers. However, if your school doesn't, you need to ask a colleague to do this for you. You could probably do it on your own, but a colleague can help you navigate the buildings smoothly. Some of the obvious places you need to locate are the principal's office, faculty restroom, student restrooms, teachers' lounge or workroom/copyroom, telephone for faculty use, cafeteria, counselor's office, library/media center, and the school nurse's office. You might also want to find the place where faculty members can make private telephone calls and the facilities that are away from the main building (e.g., music annex, agriculture complex, or technology lab).

Not only do you need a sense of where things are, but you also need to know the route your students will travel to come to your room. If a student tells you that she left homework in the music annex and that area is a great distance from your room, you may need to give the student a hall pass to use after the tardy bell has rung, or, depending on the circumstances, you may need to refuse the student's request.

LEARNING SCHOOL POLICY AND PROCEDURES

Before you begin to create lesson plans or prepare your room, you need to become familiar with school policy and procedures. Most schools have student handbooks that they make available to students, teachers, and parents. Most also have faculty handbooks for teachers and staff members. If possible, you should ask for copies of these two handbooks as soon as you know you have been hired. These documents form the structure on which you will build your career in that district. Although neither document is entertaining reading (that's why many students ignore the student handbook), you need to learn the contents of both to ensure that you know and follow the rules established by the district and to give yourself confidence in dealing with discipline. Knowing the rules and regulations before you even begin to think about classroom management and lesson plans will keep you from embarrassing situations. You don't want to require something that goes against school policy.

CREATING AN INVITING ENVIRONMENT BY ATTITUDE AND DEMEANOR

The most important aspects of creating an inviting atmosphere are your attitude and demeanor. If you are glad to be teaching, your students will know. They can tell by the look in your eyes, the tone of your voice, and the way you move about the room. They will be interested because you are interested and excited because you are excited.

Although teaching is one of the most gratifying professions in our society, not every day will be a thrilling experience. There will be days when you come to school after a sleepless night. There will be days when you are not feeling well. There will be days when problems in your personal life will weigh heavily on your shoulders. Your students will know when you are not having a good day. However, "bad" days should be greatly outnumbered by excellent days. Teachers who love what they do and truly enjoy working with students have an opportunity to make a positive difference in their students' lives and educations. Keeping that thought in mind is a basic element in creating an inviting environment.

WELCOMING STUDENTS

Your classroom should be an emotionally inviting place. If at all possible, you should be standing at the classroom door when students begin entering your room at the beginning of a period. Look each student in the eye and call him or her by name. It is possible for some students to spend the entire day without making any personal or positive contact with anyone. For example, a shy student whose parents do night-shift work may get up in the morning, have breakfast, get ready for school, and leave home without speaking one word to parents or siblings. When she gets to school, it is easy for her to avoid speaking to anyone. In your mind's eye, can you see this person? She is so shy that it is an effort for anyone to get her to speak, so it's easier for people just to ignore her. She moves from class to class all day, locked in her isolation. When the school day is over, she goes home to sleeping parents who get up in the evening and go back to work. Your greeting at the classroom door may be the only personal contact she has all day.

ANOTHER SCENARIO

Another scenario involves the belligerent student who seems to thrive on conflict. She is hateful and caustic to anyone who talks to her, and no one even wants to be around her. If you have developed the habit of greeting each student, even those who aren't lovable, you may be the only positive contact she has during the day. It can be amazing to watch both shy and belligerent students change their behavior because they know you are going to greet them and welcome them to class. Shy students begin to lift their heads and look you in the eye as they walk in the door. Before long, they will initiate the greeting if you don't. Belligerent students stop trying to instigate negative responses. They, too, begin to exchange greetings. For both types of students, that small, seemingly insignificant act of saying hello and calling their names helps them know that you are interested in them and that they are valuable to you.

Another reason it is important to greet your students is that the greeting sends a signal to troublesome students that you are giving them a second chance. There are going to be times when you will have serious problems with a student. Although you may handle the situation quickly and the issue gets resolved, quite often there will still be a feeling of resentment on either your part or the student's. It would be easy just to look away and ignore that student the next day. However, if you force yourself to look the student in the eye and give your usual greeting, the tension from the previous encounter is defused. By greeting the student, regardless of the way you may feel about the student at the moment, you have done two important things—you have acted professionally, and you have shown the student that you are an adult and are not going to hold a grudge. Greeting the student also frees you emotionally to treat him as you should. Once that greeting breaks the ice, you will feel more comfortable working with the student and giving him the help he needs.

MAKING SPACE INVITING

Your room needs to be physically inviting. Even secondary students enjoy classrooms that are decorated. As a new teacher, you will not have as much material to use as more established teachers have. However, with a little creativity, you can make your room special. Create a bulletin board that introduces you to your students. Use pictures of you with your family, friends, and pets. Cut out or print words that describe you or things you like to do. Put up a copy of your college diploma or any awards you have received. Make sure you don't use original pictures or documents. Students have an annoying habit of drawing horns and mustaches on pictures, and you don't want your originals ruined. Your students will enjoy your unusual way of introducing yourself and will get a sense of who you are. Use discretion in the things you choose to share with your students; remember that although you want to show things about yourself that make you "real" to your students, you don't want to compromise yourself professionally. Also consider the attitudes of community members where you teach. In one community it might be fine for you to display a picture of you and your friend at a casino. In another community, the same picture could generate calls from parents.

Another way to make your room physically inviting is to use things about and by students. Students like to see their names in print. Laminate a piece of colored poster board and title it "In the News." As the year progresses, cut out newspaper articles (not court reports) about your students and tape them to the poster board. As one board fills up, start another. At the end of the school year, you will have an interesting collection of information about your students, a collection they will enjoy as much as you do. You could use this information to build a scrapbook about your students. Leora, a secondary social studies teacher, selected student work, newspaper articles, and mementos (a football tossed out at the homecoming parade, a program from the band concert) each year and glued her selections to a poster board that she displayed in her room. Each year she added another poster to her room. Students enjoyed looking at the posters and recalling the events she had commemorated. They also enjoyed seeing pictures of students who had graduated in past years.

SHOW STUDENTS' WORK

It is gratifying for students to see their work displayed. Displaying student work can be rewarding and encouraging for them, but you need to keep the issue of confidentiality in mind as you choose work to use. If you are going to display graded work, cover the grade and ask the student's permission to use his work. Even if you've covered the grade, students will still be able to see your comments and identify the good things the anonymous student has done making the piece worthy of display. Again, use discretion as you choose pieces to share. You should never publicly display work that is inappropriate for school children or work that contains material that could be considered inflammatory to other groups of students. If your students know ahead of time that you are planning to display some of their papers, they are more likely to use appropriate topics and language. If they continue to write material that is inappropriate, then obviously you need to have a discussion with them outside of class to explain why the text they have written could be harmful to other students.

DISPLAY LEARNING MATERIALS

Another idea is to use learning exercises as part of a student display. At the beginning of class, give each student a 4" × 6" index card and a marker. Depending on your subject area, ask students to do the following:

- Write down one thing they enjoy as a result of the First Amendment.
- Create a mathematics problem in which the answer equals their age.
- Write a metaphor or simile for a holiday (or other special event).
- Draw a picture of their favorite crustacean.

You may ask students to sign their work or to leave their identity a mystery. You can also use the work to check students' understanding of a concept you are teaching. Discussing each piece before displaying it gives class members instant feedback on their work. For example, Mary's students enjoyed creating metaphors and similes to use on seasonal bulletin boards. Mary would cut rectangles of red, green, orange, and yellow paper and distribute them to students as they entered class. Before the tardy bell rang, she would point to a blank bulletin board that had a heading "Autumn is like. . . ." Students would write similes on their papers. After Mary finished checking role and submitting the absence report, she had students move into groups to examine their similes. If they needed to make corrections, they did so on the backs of their colored papers. Mary would collect the students' similes, check to make sure they were corrected, and staple the corrected entries on the bulletin board before the next day's class. Students enjoyed seeing what their classmates had created, and it gave Mary an opportunity to reinforce a literary device students would see in literature they would read later.

SHARED ROOMS AND SHARED DISPLAY AREAS

Sometimes teachers have to share rooms with each other. That makes decorating a room more of a challenge. Instead of decorating the entire room, you might ask for the use of one wall or a part of a wall. If you travel from room to room, you might ask for a portion of a wall just for your class that meets in that room. Although it might involve a little more effort to create displays for more than one room, investing the time will let your students know that they are important to you and that you value their work and ideas enough to share them with others. They must always know that each one of them is special.

GETTING TO KNOW
YOUR COLLEAGUES

You will find that you are an automatic member in some groups. For example, if your district is large enough to have several teachers in your subject area, you will be part of that subject-area group. If you are assigned to help sponsor organizations or activities, you will find yourself part of another group. Sometimes becoming part of a faculty is a little intimidating. Teachers who have taught and worked together for a few years may be so comfortable and secure that they have forgotten what it's like to be a new teacher. Don't sit back and wait to be included. In group sessions, try to sit with people you think you would like to get to know. Ask questions and accept advice. You don't need to be intrusive or thrust your opinion on the group, but if you indicate an interest in what your colleagues are doing and saying, they will be apt to include you in their conversations. Sometimes it is lonely as you wait to be accepted, but try to remember that forming relationships takes time and effort.

Many jokes are told about teachers who "hang out" in the teachers' lounge. It seems to be a common perception that these people are only interested in gossiping rather than working. That is not always the case. Many times the informal atmosphere in the teachers' lounge makes it possible to socialize and get to know your colleagues. As with everything else, balance is the key to success. If you find yourself engaging in gossip or using your planning period exclusively for socializing, evaluate why you are spending so much time there and make whatever adjustments you need to make to behave as a professional.

GETTING TO KNOW YOUR MENTOR

Many states and school districts assign new teachers to a mentor teacher. The mentor is responsible for disseminating information and guiding the new teacher through the first year in that district. When this policy works well, the new teacher feels less isolated and less unsure of what to do. The mentor can help with everything from how to handle classroom management issues and what to do with difficult students to what to expect for a special emphasis week. He can help the new teacher to negotiate curriculum and state mandates while also observing in the classroom and providing encouragement and advice. Many times the mentor becomes a lifelong friend and confidant.

Sometimes the mentor and mentee do not hold similar views and philosophies on teaching and learning. That can be a potential problem, depending on the amount of input the mentor has in questions of certification. In some states, the mentor is on the certification committee responsible for helping the new teacher meet the state's certification requirements. In states where the mentor is required to spend a specified number of hours observing the first-year teacher and to be closely involved in evaluating teaching methods, this mentor may be the pivotal member of the committee on certification issues. You might be able to request that another mentor be assigned to you if your views and philosophies are in conflict, but if the district is small, there may not be other teachers who are qualified. If it is impossible for you to be assigned to another mentor, you will need to make the best of the situation for the ensuing year. Remember, however, that even though you may not agree with your mentor, he may have good reasons for his beliefs and practices. Maybe he has tried some things the way you would like to try them and has found from experience that they will not work in that district or with those students. Maybe he insists on doing things a certain way because they have worked well for him and he thinks you should try them as well. Regardless of why you don't agree with him, try to turn a potentially negative experience into a positive one. Even though you may disagree, you can still learn from your mentor, and you must respect his experience and views.

If the state or school where you teach does not provide mentoring, it would be well worth your time to find someone who would agree to be your unofficial mentor. For example, many professional organizations such as the National Writing Project offer mentoring as part of their work with teachers. In the event that you cannot find a professional organization, forming a group with former classmates via e-mail might be a viable alternative. If your university supervisor is not overwhelmed, she might agree to keep in touch with you during the first year. The point is this: The first year is full of challenges. Having someone to share these challenges with will give you more self-assurance as you navigate your first year in the classroom. Don't be afraid to ask for help. Asking for help is not an admission of incompetence; it is an indication that you want to do a good job.

GETTING TO KNOW
OTHER STAFF MEMBERS

Another important step is to meet staff members. Sometimes they are not available to attend the faculty meetings at the beginning of the year. However, they are an important part of the total system. For example, the secretaries are valuable sources of information. They can help you with many of the details that are part of teaching—when grade reports are due, where to find textbooks, how to request supplies, what procedures to use in contacting parents, and so forth. Some of the most frustrating moments for a new teacher are when faculty members have failed to explain something simply because they are all so familiar with the routine that they have forgotten that the new faculty members need help. Jennifer found herself in an awkward position the first semester of her new job. Instead of building a relationship with a slightly intimidating school secretary, Jennifer avoided Ms. Smith. She didn't realize that her actions were interpreted as snobbery. The school did not assign mentor teachers to new personnel, and because she was shy, Jennifer decided to keep to herself. The sixth week of school was Homecoming Week. Jennifer read the announcement that listed a special emphasis for each day of the week—hat day, school spirit day, cowboy day, fifties day, wear your colors day, and crazy day. That's all the information that the office had given. Because nothing was said about special activities during those days, Jennifer planned an instructional video one day, group project work the next day, and then ended the week with an essay test. No one told her that classes would be cut short on Wednesday so that students could participate in a schoolwide picnic. Nor did anyone tell her that although classes were scheduled all day on Friday, the cheerleaders, band members, pep club, and all float entry participants would be dismissed at noon to prepare for the parade. When Jennifer realized that one of the other new teachers knew all about the chaos of Homecoming Week, she asked why she hadn't been informed. Her colleague shrugged his shoulders. The following week, he stopped Jennifer in the hallway. "What have you done to make Ms. Smith mad?" he asked. "I overheard her tell someone that if you hadn't been so rude to her, she would have made sure you knew all about Homecoming?" It wasn't until that moment that Jennifer understood that her shyness had been misinterpreted.

Custodians are another excellent source of help. They know where you can find ladders, chalkboard cleaner, mops, and paper towels. They can find extra desks and repair those that are broken. They can also tell you where to find dollies and carts for moving books and equipment. A politely worded request may result in their helping you with anything from moving desks to cleaning up after a sick student.

It is so important for a first year teacher to understand that often support staff feel intimidated by their college-educated colleagues. Small acts of kindness and a heartfelt "thank you" go a long way in bridging that gap and creating a partnership that benefits students.

DISCOVERING THE "THOU SHALT/THOU SHALT NOTS"

One of the most difficult things for a new teacher is discovering all of the unspoken rules that exist in the school. This can be especially difficult if experienced teachers don't follow policy and procedure, giving the impression that rules don't matter. For the new faculty members, it is imperative to follow carefully the procedures that are identified in the student handbook and the faculty handbook. Even if you feel that you are the only one going by the book, it is better for you to err on the side of doing what is required than to be reprimanded for being out of line. Realize that reprimands are documented and become a part of your professional file.

Faculties seem to be divided into three general groups—those who never follow the rules, those who bend the rules occasionally, and those who never bend or break the rules. Quite often, you may feel a real temptation to bend or break the rules. Students can be so persistent in their requests and make you think they would really like you so much better if you would just break a rule or two. The truth is that if you insist on following the rules and do so with a good attitude, the students will respect you much more than they do the teachers who try to act as their buddies and ignore the rules. Even more important, perhaps, the teacher who is known for following the rules is less likely to be involved in a situation that results in a lawsuit or termination.

LISTENING CAREFULLY AND OBSERVING CLOSELY

During your first year in a new school, it is imperative that you learn to listen carefully and observe closely. In a few weeks you will know who the master teachers are in your building. Watch what they do, and listen to what they say. If you have not been assigned a mentor teacher to guide you through the first year, choose one of the master teachers whose personality seems compatible with yours. Ask him if you may come to him with questions about what you should and should not do. Usually a teacher is flattered when a new teacher makes such a request. It is possible that the master teacher will take the responsibility of seeing that the new faculty member is informed not only about day-to-day activities but also about what the administration expects from faculty members in every kind of situation.

FINDING YOUR NICHE

The first year in a school can be a lonely time for a new teacher. If you are in your 20s and have just completed college, you will probably feel more comfortable socializing with students than with faculty members. You might prefer to sit at a table in the cafeteria with your students rather than sit with the faculty. However uncomfortable you feel in your new role as a faculty member, you must make the transition from student to teacher immediately. Developing friendships with students must be avoided—*with no exceptions.* Once you cross the line from teacher to friend, you have compromised your authority and possibly your integrity. Students are flattered by attention from young teachers. Many times what seems like an innocent friendship to the teacher is a completely different relation-ship in the eyes of a student. This is especially true with students of the opposite sex. Any action of a teacher that could be construed as flirting is inappropriate. As a member of a faculty, a new teacher must realize that she has stepped into an adult world. Things that she considered acceptable only a few months or weeks ago are now professionally off limits. A young teacher must keep in mind the fragility of teenage egos and the danger inherent in encouraging students to become friends. Friendships between faculty and students can only lead to problems, and often those problems can lead to the teacher's termination. Always keep in mind that once you have signed a contract with a district, you have accepted the responsibilities of a teacher. You must behave as a professional and insist that students accept you as a professional. Before long you will find yourself more comfortable with your status as classroom teacher and will find your niche in the new environment.

REMAINING FLEXIBLE

You may be surprised at what you do *not* find in your first teaching experience. Some of the resources you had at your disposal in student teaching may not exist. The importance of students' social life may surprise you. The myriad interruptions to your classes may distress you. Learn to take a deep breath and do the best you can do in the situation. The longer you teach, the more easily you will be able to handle the milieu of teaching in the secondary set-ting. Remember that part of your responsibility is to prepare these young people to be successful in the world outside your classroom. That will make it a little easier to tolerate all of the interruptions that creep into your instruction—at least some of the time.

JOURNAL TOPICS

- What are some questions you would like to have answered before you meet with your first class?
- Brainstorm some ideas for using student work in your subject area to enhance your room.
- List some behaviors that could compromise your being con-sidered a "teacher" rather than a student.

CHAPTER TWO

Surviving Requires Working Well With Students

Teaching is a wonderfully complex endeavor. You read, study, and plan so that you can instruct. This preparation and instruction is such a small part of the art of teaching, however. You will learn quickly that to be successful, you must know not only your subject matter but also your students. Young people are an ever-evolving, ever-changing group. They are so much more sophisticated about the world in which they live than students of even just a few years ago. If you were a traditional college student, you might be only 4 years removed from the young people you will be teaching, and you may be closer to knowing what they feel and know about the world than someone further removed. If you happen to be one of that rapidly growing set of nontraditional students who decided to return to school later in life to become a teacher, you may be startled at how sophisticated your students are, whether they are in middle school or secondary school. Young people are just much more involved in the world than their predecessors were at the same ages.

EXAMINING POSTMODERNISM IN THINKING ABOUT STUDENTS

Preservice teachers so often bemoan so much of their professional education's being focused on theory. They want more hands-on experiences and nuts-and-bolts information about how to succeed in the classroom, how to teach, and how to manage students. But a strong theory base is required so that if a plan doesn't work well, there is something more waiting to be tried. The importance of operating from a theory base may not be apparent until after a person has entered the profession. Identifying a theory as a basis of practice gives a teacher a way to examine what happens in the classroom in the context of the larger picture of learning and learners. It helps a teacher to be successful in understanding how the world outside impacts the culture inside the classroom. The postmodern theory described by Doll (1993) and Linn (1996) is a theory that fits well with trends seen in learning and teaching practices today. Doll and Linn describe the era into which the world is moving as one lacking in traditional families, traditional values, traditional responses, and therefore traditional learning. Doll describes this era as the "age of chaos." He says that teachers in such a world must accept each student's differences; each needs an individually tailored learning plan. This trend can be seen in the increased number of individual education plans teachers are designing for special needs students. Designing individually appropriate lessons not only for those identified with special needs but for all students could effectively change the course of today's teaching. Evidence can be seen of a movement toward such teaching in brain research and in research on learning styles and multiple intelligences. Teachers must avail themselves of the opportunity to read and make theory trials so that their students become the best instructed they can be.

The postmodern teacher must now be accountable for addressing students with special needs, addressing state- and district-mandated curriculum, and meeting the needs of students with a language other than English. All of these tasks include designing a classroom management system that fosters responsibility and independence and developing methodologies to meet those responsibilities, such as a differentiated classroom that reflects on the quality of the material that is being differentiated. The differentiated classroom focuses on the needs of individuals within the classroom, and although at first that seems an impossible task, all of it can be done with careful planning. We will discuss this in detail in Chapter 4.

The postmodern teacher will develop a different learning relationship with his students. He will not walk up and down traditional rows of students, for instance. Instead, there will be a great deal of interactivity and group work in progress most of the time, so he will walk among groups steeped in subject matter and discovery and working toward solving a problem that each group has recognized as needing solving. The teacher will be more than a lecturer or dispenser of knowledge. He has to become a facilitator who will help to keep students focused on the learning objectives for each lesson, yet work at an individualized pace so that each student's needs are met rather than the desires or plans of the teacher. He will need to incorporate tried-and-true methods as well as new ideas. He must be constantly looking for those new ideas as ways to connect with his students and to make learning meaningful to them. The foundation for meeting the needs of students is to know those students truly.

The postmodern educator will give batteries of diagnostic tests to determine where her students are in their cognitive development. She can determine the profile of each learner in her classroom. She can do inventories to check on whether the student is an analytic, dynamic, intuitive, or commonsense learner so that she can group students according to their "work" differentiation. She can observe the learners to determine whether they are visual, auditory, kinesthetic, or tactile learners. She can set up work in the proper environment to meet the needs of individual students. She can pull all of this information together so that she can differentiate her lessons to fit the needs of her students. There are many different personality profile inventories to aid the teacher in getting to these facts so that the counselor in the system, or perhaps the principal, can make suggestions to fit these needs within individual schools.

Postmodern teachers need to know their students well enough to know what kind of material to provide to them to maintain maximum growth (maturation) and achievement for their grade level. The postmodern teacher has to know his or her students' stories. William Kilpatrick (1993) says in his now almost classic book *Why Johnny Can't Tell Right From Wrong: And What We Can Do About It* that teachers and parents have far too long neglected the "story." He cautions that "life is a story." If teachers are to succeed with getting their students ready to compete in, or really, even to get them ready to participate in, this rapidly approaching postmodern age, they must know the students' stories and be able to teach their subject matter in such a way that students' stories may be applied, so that students will care about what is being studied (authenticity).

It is no longer a good plan when Johnny asks, "Why do we have to study this? It's boring. Who cares?" for a teacher to answer, "Because it is in the plan or because it is one of *my* favorite things," or "Because it is in the textbook."

One fledgling teacher tells the story of his freshman English student who sat in the classroom the second week of school humming, drawing doodles, sighing loudly, and twisting and turning restlessly in her desk.

The teacher asked, "What is your problem?"

The girl responded instantly:

Why do we have to study Sir Arthur Conan Doyle? We know he wrote about Sherlock Holmes. You told us that yesterday. You told us about Watson, his sidekick. They solved crimes. I could have solved the crime using the same logic that they had in a couple of days, and we have been reading him for 7 days. If I can't use what you are teaching, why are you teaching it? Can't we study something more interesting to us? What is school for, anyway, the teachers' enjoyment?

The teacher had a difficult time responding. Where does such material fit into the "authenticity" factor? Could the teacher have made the application by using some current newspaper case of murder and applying the techniques of Holmes and Watson? In fact, the same question of the value of the piece arose in his mind. Why was this particular piece placed in the textbook of literature that he was using? Many new teachers think that because a text has information in it, the class must cover that material. For universal coverage, it is true that certain materials will be covered in the standardized tests that are given each year, but that does not mean that every piece of the text has to be explicated to the stage of utter despair and boredom to both the teacher and the students. In this case, the Sherlock Holmes piece could have been mentioned with highlighted passages to substantiate Holmes' inventive crime solving, and it could also have been taught along with some modern young adult piece of literature.

Not to belabor the point too much, but even though Doyle is a good writer, his nineteenth-century vocabulary and settings are not relevant in most of today's classrooms. When even the best students cannot grasp the words and situations, the teacher must decide what to teach most effectively. To broaden student appreciation of Doyle, perhaps the teacher could have the students work in groups and determine what a select passage means by paraphrasing it. Each group could have a different passage to explicate, then when each group gives an oral presentation on their updated Holmes passage, the entire class can benefit. Of course, the teacher moves from group to group to be certain that the material is being assimilated by all the members of the group. Each group member should have something to contribute orally as a part of that group's demonstration. (We discuss this in Chapter 4 in more detail.)

RECOGNIZING DIFFERENT TYPES OF STUDENTS

You have heard much about this notion in your professional education classes. As you get into the "real" world of having your own set of students and the responsibility of reaching your own students with your vast array of knowledge, you may need to be reminded of some of the factors you may face. Many of the students you will be teaching come from nontraditional family units. They may not have the parental support that is necessary to keep them interested or motivated to stay in school. Many times their parents are working long hours to provide survival for them and their families. Sometimes these parents become so involved in earning a living, or just in living, that they don't have time to see the various needs of their children. Often, the children are thought to be more "adult" and secure than they, in fact, are. Often it is the case that if their teachers are not encouraging them to stay in school, they may just drop out. These *at-risk* students come from every socioeconomic group, from every ethnic group, though statistics reveal that some groups have higher percentages dropping out of school (Burden & Byrd, 1994), and from the largest to the smallest of communities—from every kind of life and home. But all of them are the students whom we, as teachers, must understand and with whom we must work to bring about learning so that these students may become more adult and secure.

AT-RISK STUDENTS NEED ATTENTION

Many at-risk students do not have the content tools they need to be successful in school. Students most likely to drop out are those who are not up to grade level in basic reading, verbal, and mathematical skills. Many have behavioral problems, often based on deficient content knowledge. Family values often do not place a high enough emphasis on education (Moore, 1999). Many parents, themselves dropouts, will push their children's staying in school by saying, "One thing that they can't take from you is an education." But many parents also are so involved in their own convoluted worlds that either they don't know that their children have dropped out of school or they just don't care. Parents agree that they, like their children, just can't handle the "hassle" every day. They have other problems, which at the time seem more pressing than having to deal with the school attendance of their children.

You will have special students of several other kinds, too. There are those who are busy working 40 hours a week to make the payments on their vehicles. There are those who have social needs that keep them from going to bed and getting sufficient rest. There are those who have alcohol or drug-related problems. There are those who are married and have, or are expecting, a child. Many students have little support outside themselves, but they want to "do the right thing." There are also those who have low self-esteem, and because they have always been told that they cannot accomplish something, believe it, or perhaps when they have accomplished beyond a parent's or teacher's expectations, have not been praised enough to realize the value of their accomplishments. These are some of the students you will have in your classroom, no matter where you teach.

THE STUDIOUS NEED HELP

You will also have what have come to be known as "geeks" or "nerds." They will be just as uninspired, perhaps, by what you have to offer them, as those who are troubled or troublesome. They will be in every level of environment in which you might find yourself. They are the ones who are teased and tormented by some of the other types. With these students, you will need to teach content, but you will also need to teach social skills. You need to create an environment where their abilities are appreciated and where they have a chance to feel accepted and nourished.

POPULAR STUDENTS ARE AT RISK

You will also have the "social butterflies" and the "climbers" who spend all their time trying to be popular and impress their peers. They have needs that are omnipresent, and you may have to deal with those needs in your classroom, no matter what you teach. When dealing with adolescents, you have to remember that their social lives are inherently bound up in their educational lives. They are shortsighted, and social problems that seem minute to an adult can be extremely traumatic for the young person. For example, a sobbing teenage girl comes to class distraught because she has just caught her boyfriend and her best friend kissing, and based on her past behavior, you know that the child will have a new boyfriend before the day is over. You will need to learn how to handle the emotional crises of one student while you press on to your goals and objectives for the whole class. Our theory training gives us that kind of capability. All we have to do is apply that knowledge that is part of our training.

No amount of theory-based education classes can prepare you for the multiple problems and realities you will face, often on a daily basis. The No Child Left Behind legislation is an enigma for all educators. Pressures develop when this kind of law is enacted. A constant question that generates many good, emotional discussions, is "How can we accomplish such a feat?"

Each teacher is required to be highly qualified to teach all the children and bring them all up to a specified capability according to their grade level. When faced with the question of how that may be accomplished in our individual classrooms and still teach all the material that we want to teach, frustration ensues. Many teachers feel as if they just need to quit thinking something like "I cannot accomplish the impossible."

A new teacher in a small rural school called the first author and said, "How can I possibly do plans for five secondary classroom preparations, help coach the football team, and make any headway toward getting all of my students up to their specified ability levels?"

Bob's advice was for the teacher to gather the school's, the state's, and the nation's standards for his subject matters for the grade levels that he teaches. Bob told him that no one ever said that teaching would be easy. He reminded the new teacher of the theoretical base of constructivist philosophy of building on what a student knows, moving always upward on the scaffolding of learning and that this theory had carried this teacher through some very difficult certification tests. Bob reminded the teacher that he had passed these tests and was now a highly qualified expert in his subject matter. Bob reassured the new teacher that he was well versed in his subject and in his pedagogy. Finally, Bob reminded him of the important adage that "less is more," and reiterated that studying the standards allowed the new teacher to choose the items that he believed to be the more important items that his class must study. Bob's encouragement reminded the new teacher that his high qualification gave him the authority to make the final decision of exactly what he should cover with his classes.

It turned out that the new teacher admitted that he had just not done much planning, just writing page numbers in the text in his short lesson plans. Bob reminded him again of the importance of allowing the students' needs to help him differentiate his materials to meet their needs. They discussed once again peer teaching (kids working in small groups to assure that they are getting information from the textual material), peer demonstrations, peer construction, and peer writing (this is covered in detail in Chapter 4).

Such teaching, as the teacher recalled from his pedagogy classes in the education department, also allows the teacher to meet the special needs students' individual education plan (IEP) requirements. Teachers must assure that the IEP goals are met. It is true that special needs students are basically the only students with special plans dictated by their needs, as stated in the IEPs. The postmodernist, however, understands that basically every student must have individualized goal or objectives to meet in every lesson. This kind of goal-setting or objective-setting can be accomplished by talking with the students and having them help determine what they can apply from the material that the teacher feels compelled to teach. This leads to authenticity, and once the lessons become authentic to each student, then the student will learn.

THE NEW AT-RISK STUDENT

Then there are those traditional types who, if they don't excel at all that they do, will at least try to do all that you ask of them. They are not your discipline problems. They don't mind how you teach them. They will listen to the traditional lecture. They will do the worksheets that you provide. They will accomplish their seatwork and homework on a somewhat regular basis. They will nod their heads as if they are getting the material, and most likely, they really are, but often just don't care to share it. Their parents will come to meet with you if you ask. They will be the ones on whom you will generally more easily shower your attention. They are the ones that you are so happy to have in your classroom on days when you just don't feel like being motivational or inspirational. They will perform as expected, regardless. But, in fact, they may also be at risk. If educators are, indeed, moving into an age of postmodernism, they must meet these students' needs also. These compliant students will reach the short-term goals, just as they traditionally have; but will they be lifelong learners or lifelong carriers of what you have taught them? Lifelong learning is another of those goals toward which the new generation of teachers must learn to push. We must give all the students some material to carry away with them.

TEACHING STUDENTS
WITH SPECIAL NEEDS

Since 1975, Public Law 94-142 (Kellough, 1999) has mandated that youngsters with various exceptionalities have rights of education that give teachers an opportunity to include them in the regular classroom activities. These students work under individualized educational plans (IEP) (Kellough, 1999) that give them work assignments on the basis of their assessed needs and capabilities.

According to this law, students with special needs are placed in the least restrictive learning environment possible. That means that the classroom teacher may have to adjust strategies and teaching styles to accommodate some students. So many times when a teacher learns that she will have a child with special needs in her class, she reacts with disgust or irritation—usually as a result of being unsure of what is required to meet the needs of these students. Remember that if the student were your child, you would want the best education possible for him. If you can keep that in mind, making accommodations and concessions seems less inconvenient. Ironically, that may be the very student you reach the most in your endeavors. You must follow each student's IEP to the letter. It is your responsibility, and it is a legal requirement.

Because many students with severe disabilities can't function in the regular classroom, you will probably not have any of these students in your classes. You may, however, have students in wheelchairs or with other special apparatus such as hearing aids, seeing-eye dogs, or technological aids. To help these students function in your classroom, you need to do simple things such as rearrange desks, assign students to help the disabled students move from place to place, stand so that you are in their line of vision when you speak to the class, or speak louder when talking to the class.

These young people will want to be as unobtrusive as possible. A student in one of Maria's junior English classes was paraplegic as a result of a car accident she had on her 16th birthday. Maria assigned her the desk at the front of the row by the door, thinking it wouldn't take her so much time to enter and leave the classroom. However, when the class did group work, the student would always wheel herself over to the other side of the room and squeeze her wheelchair between the rows of desks. After watching her do this for several days, Maria asked her if she would like the group to move over to her desk. She looked up quickly, frowning, and snapped, "No! I can get over there just fine, and besides that, I don't like it over here!" What her teacher hadn't realized was that by assigning this student to an area close to the door, she had created a situation in which the student felt she was in everyone's way as they entered or left the room. The student felt more secure on the opposite side of the classroom where other students didn't have to walk around her wheelchair to leave or enter class. Such a minor item of classroom arrangement is one of the basic thoughts that a teacher must have when beginning a teaching career. This doesn't seem a big issue to the teacher, but to the student, it may be a problem of immense proportion.

STUDENTS WITH SPECIAL NEEDS ON FIELD TRIPS

When taking students with special needs on field trips, you will need to think ahead to determine how you will help them participate in a way that is physically and emotionally comfortable for them. For example, a choir director who had a student with a physical challenge made arrangements for her choir to perform on the floor in front of the stage at a district contest so that the student, who was in a wheelchair, could sing with the group. There were no ramps or street-level doors that opened to the stage area. Rather than having the student sit down on the floor to perform while the rest of the choir stood on risers, the director in advance of the concert requested permission from the judges to change the performance area. When it came time for the choir members to sing, they walked down to the front of the auditorium, arranged themselves in the proper places, and sang as if what they were doing was the norm. The student in the wheelchair sat up as straight as possible, watched the director intently, and participated fully with the other choir members.

Sometimes it is easier to make accommodations for students with physical challenges than it is to make modifications of lessons for students with learning disabilities. Because students with learning disabilities function more like other students, it may be difficult for a teacher to realize that they need help; they are disabled in a way that is not visible. In schools with good special education programs, teachers from the special education department communicate frequently with the regular classroom teachers to help them learn how to provide effective instruction for these special needs students with the modification procedures. Sometimes all the regular teacher needs to do is something as simple as allowing a child with learning disabilities more time to complete a task, or sending her to the special education teacher to take a test orally that the other students will take written. Sometimes the problem can be addressed by the teacher's making shorter assignments or changing the grading criteria slightly to modify the learning for the student (Moore, 1999).

STUDENTS WITH SPECIAL NEEDS PROVIDE UNIQUE CHALLENGES

Students with learning disabilities provide unique challenges for their teachers. These students often have symptoms that are so like behavior problems (Moore, 1999) that it is difficult for a teacher to separate the child from the actions (Kellough, 1999). Some of these students are also extremely bright and learn quickly how to manipulate teachers to make it seem as if the assignment is too hard or too long. It is important for a classroom teacher to rely heavily on the teachers in the special education department. Special education teachers, trained specifically to deal with this kind of student, can be invaluable in helping a classroom teacher understand the difficulties these children have with some teaching strategies and in devising strategies to help the students succeed in the regular classroom. Another reason a special education teacher is so valuable is that a trained specialist knows when a student is trying to manipulate a classroom teacher, and he or she can help a classroom teacher curb these manipulations.

You may have heard horror stories about the difficulties teachers have had with special needs children. While it is true that horror stories happen, they are very rare. Usually, you have to make only small changes to meet disabled students' needs. One thing you should remember in dealing with all students with special needs is that your attitude and actions will be reflected in the attitudes and actions of your students. If you resent the extra time and effort you are compelled to expend with students with any kinds of disabilities, your other students will know that. If, however, you use the situation as a way to learn how to relate to and help students with special needs, your class will have an opportunity to learn a great deal about tolerance and compassion. Your actions and attitude will be mirrored by your students. Working with students with special needs is potentially a rich learning experience for everyone.

Ben had a special opportunity to work with secondary special education students, teaching to prepare and present a personal portfolio. When he visited the special education classroom, he took along with him some examples of portfolios assigned to his college students as one of the alternative assessments for his students. He also took along his own professional portfolio. He instructed them as to how to construct a portfolio, which took several class periods (see Chapter 4). Some of the students were going to do little more than prepare scrapbooks. Others had decided to make their portfolios a preparation to show to prospective employers. Some did portfolios showing their academic learning performance. The type of portfolio that each made was up to him or her. All of them—some with more help from the classroom paraprofessionals, the teachers, and Ben—created portfolios. Once the basic instruction was done, the students worked on their own in the classroom, with teacher supervision, to complete their portfolio projects. When they were all done, the class invited Ben back for their oral presentations of their portfolios. They were extremely proud of their work. They could not all speak for themselves due to a disability or stage fright, but as the teacher or the paraprofessional spoke for these students, the preparing student held his or her portfolio and showed the page being discussed.

After 15 years have passed, the students will occasionally see Ben and tell him how good that portfolio experience was for them. One of the students said, "I still keep it up every time I accomplish something." Another said, "I think that portfolio that you helped me make got me into my college classes, and I graduated with an associate's degree. I plan to even get a bachelor's." Another said,

I took my portfolio to my first job interview, and I got hired because the boss could see that I had a good experience record. I put a list of all my jobs in my portfolio, and pictures my mom made of me working in each one of those places.

No one in the area had ever thought to have them make their own portfolios in a special education class 15 years ago, but now portfolios are often used as special education alternative assessment tools.

WELCOMING STUDENTS WITH LIMITED ENGLISH PROFICIENCY

Another aspect of student understanding is to be aware of the number of students with limited English proficiency that you have in your school. This is a factor that is growing rapidly in larger cities and in places where farm workers have migrated into an area to work. Recent figures show that there are as many as 2.1 million students within this category (Orlich, Harder, Callahan, & Gibson, 2001). With good awareness of the problem that speakers of other languages have with English, a teacher can make her classroom one in which these students can feel somewhat at ease. Many of the students will speak nonstandard English at home, too. They may feel intimidated by standard English, but with careful planning and good modeling, that issue can become one that does not cause the student too much pain. The teacher has to understand the need for students' autonomy and pride in their upbringing and be very careful not to try to take away that pride. If at all possible, enlist the help of a professional—a student, teacher, or parent who is fluent in the language your students speak. Find ways for them to translate your instructions and the limited English proficiency students' work. Help the class learn words from those students' vocabularies. Find books about their culture to share with their new classmates. Regardless of the fact that the secondary or middle school student may not fully understand all that the teacher says, the two can still develop mutual respect if the student understands that the teacher is interested in her new student and the culture from which he comes.

COOPERATIVE LEARNING AND INDIVIDUALIZED LESSONS

This specialized instructional need is something that the teacher with a postmodern perspective will understand. The theory of learning in a chaotic era is not frightening because it fosters having students working at their own speeds all the time. A trend of the future, perhaps because of so much home schooling and specialized charter schooling, is to bring about individualized instruction to all students. Cooperative learning has the potential to meet the needs of many learners (Moore, 2005; Ornstein, 1990). By allowing students to work in groups focused on producing a result (e.g., group consensus about a topic, a project developed and prepared by the group, topics for further study), they are able to use their strengths for the work of the group while they receive help in their weaker abilities. Students access different learning styles and incorporate different intelligences (we discuss this in Chapter 4). A teacher who takes the time to train his students in effective cooperative learning strategies has provided an instructional tool that makes learning authentic, relevant, and enjoyable. He also provides the students with a social skill that they will carry with them throughout their lives. Most people have to deal with groups in their life encounters. This socialization process is a part of the postmodern viewpoint. The ability to work with other people makes our daily living so much more rewarding.

WHERE DO YOU START?

One of the first things that you must do once school starts is to find out some things about your students as quickly as you can. You can do this through your introductions. One good approach is for the teacher to have 3" × 5" index cards with him on that first day of class. He can give the students a card and ask them to record on the horizontal and lined side of the card their names, circling or putting in parentheses the name they prefer to be called. Next, he should ask them to write three facts about themselves that would help him and the other students remember the names of everyone in the class. Then, the teacher can challenge each person in the room to listen to these recorded cues for name recollection. Ask the students to try to name all those introduced; tell them that they could get bonus points for the very first week of school if they know the names and one or two facts about each of the students in the room. One of the best things about this activity is that it indicates that all students are important, not just those who are popular or outgoing.

Another method of introducing each other is to have each student introduce another student in the room. This is a strategy of interviewing and discussing that begins to build camaraderie and trust from the very beginning. Perhaps brainstorming with the class for the kind of information to seek in the interview is a good technique for critical thinking, too. We have to know what we want to know so that we can find that which we seek. If you have a real time constraint, perhaps the teacher could have a set of questions drawn up so that each interviewee would be asked the same questions. Some questions might revolve around hobbies, games, interests, and families. Another idea that could be a point of interest would be asking what the student's favorite movie is and why he or she likes it (or the favorite television show and why, the favorite piece of music and why, etc.). Another question could be about the interviewee's favorite foods. What are the interviewee's aspirations for the future? What kinds of things does the interviewee enjoy reading? From these questions and answers, interviewer students should have jotted notes and compiled an introduction that would be presented during the next time the class meets. Once the students get to know each other and you get to know them, your class will have fewer difficulties. Students care about their lives and the lives of their peers. They appreciate the teacher asking something about their personal likes and dislikes occasionally.

Everyone, even someone who claims otherwise, chooses to have a name. Each one prefers to be called by something rather than "you in the second seat, second row." Sometimes, we teachers hate to use nicknames, but if that is the name the student prefers or has gone by all his life, why not? Ted, a new science teacher, commented in the lounge one day that he hated to use the nickname of one of the boys in his class who was known as Booger. Ted asked if the young man wouldn't prefer to be called by his real name, Booth, or even something else. His reply was quick: "I answer to Booger, and if you call me anything else, I probably wouldn't know who you was [sic] calling on." So, Ted had a Booger in his classroom instead of a Booth, even though, honestly, Booger might have been called on more frequently had he used another name. Ted said when talking about it one day, "I am only human!"

Now, if that method doesn't work for you or you are embarrassed by using a nickname, you can certainly use the more traditional, rule-book approach, but Booger, Petey, Chopper, Cat, Frizzy, and Cassie might not be as ready to respond to you if you insist on using their official names as they might otherwise have been. One rather stuffy, traditional teacher called each of his students Miss or

Mister Jones or whatever their last names were. The students laughed at his ultraconservatism, even if they didn't mind his method.

Engage your students in conversation between classes. Speak to them in the halls. Attend their sports events and other extracurricular activities. If you let them know that your interest in them goes beyond their names and a few interesting facts, they will begin to respond to you in positive ways. Everyone likes to be known, and the teacher who gets to know his students in wholesome ways will lay the groundwork for a relationship of trust and mutual respect.

ESTABLISHING MUTUAL TRUST

One way to have an effective journal writing experience is to give each student a 4" × 6" index card. Ask them to number from 1 to 25 on the lines of the card. Then ask them to brainstorm memories of their past, telling them to keep the list of memories away from illegal activities, very personal religious experiences, politics, and anything hurtful to another person. As you come to journal writing time, you assign all students to write that day about the memory referred to on number 22 of their list. All of the writings will be different, but each should certainly have something to say about the student's own personal memories. The instruction is to ask them to tell a story about their memory. They should write from their own memory bank and use as much of the class time as the teacher allots for this exercise. If they haven't time to complete the exercise they might be allowed to take the journal home to complete the assignment. Tell them that you will call for volunteers to share their journal entries on a prescribed day. Most will do well on this kind of thought generator because they each have stories to tell.

One of Bob's students wrote this story (paraphrased here):

Yesterday's sermon really hit home for me. I go to a church that frowns on too much makeup and too many frills about life. We still hear periodic sermons on makeup and shorts that are too short and dyed or bleached hair. I had asked to get some makeup, especially eye makeup and lipstick and rouge, but my mom and grandma, who lives with us, had both said that I was too young to wear it. So I had to bow to their wishes.

The preacher was really preaching away in our conservative little church, and he looked right at one of our old members who always wore makeup, sometimes perhaps more than she really needed to make a statement. As he looked at her, he said, "You can paint an old barn, but it is still an old barn." Everyone in the congregation knew whom he was talking about. There was kind of a united gasp, and everyone knew the preacher was in trouble for attacking this old saint who just happened to like to wear makeup.

After his sermon, as the woman walked out the door, she shook the preacher's hand just as cordially as she always did, and she said, "Preacher, that was a good sermon for the most part. I do have a comment about one of your illustrations." Everyone tuned in on the speaker. She added," I have been around for more than eighty years. I have seen a good many old barns in all those years, but I have never seen an old barn that didn't look better with a coat of paint." (Wyatt, 1990, p. 19)

The class laughed and really enjoyed her journal story—after reading it and enjoying it so much himself, Bob had asked if the student would share with the others. She got such a thrill from writing that story listed as number 22 on her memory card. She has completed her degree and is now a professional writer. She says that this journal exercise and the listeners' interest in it were the genesis of her professional career.

As the weeks progress, you might get to know your students better through their writing journals. Elizabeth, a new civics teacher, had her students write in a journal each day so that they could do some writing across the curriculum (Tompkins, 1998). She had them write either at the beginning of class so they would be busy as she called the roll or did other housekeeping chores, or at the end of the period to keep them engaged in meaningful activity right up until the bell rang. They wrote frequently in English class, but not so frequently in science or math or even social studies. She occasionally asked them to write on some generic topics, but she also asked them on some days to share themselves in some way. She told them that she would read the material that they wrote but that she would not share anything from their journals with anyone else unless they wrote about something illegal or potentially harmful to them. In those cases, she told them, she would have to notify some authority figure. She later said that she found off-the-cuff kind of writing was very revealing to her concerning her students' personalities and character. She agreed that she had to be ready to learn more, really, than she might otherwise have wanted to know, and she had to maintain the pledge that she would not, under any circumstances, other than the disclaimers already stated, reveal anything they had written to *any* other person (including parents, friends, principals, counselors, and teacher lounge–lizards) without the students' permission. A teacher, and especially a new one who wishes to be effective, must establish a bond of trust. The student will surely try you out, too, to see if you can be trusted to keep the confidentiality of the journal as you promised. Those journals become depositories for all kinds of language, dialogue, and situations. If you are the least bit squeamish about knowing your students, don't assign and read their journals. However, if you truly want to know your students, a journal is perhaps the best way to do so.

JOURNALS REVEAL WARM THOUGHTS

Journals are the best source for you to get to know and establish trust with your students. Journal writing is a way in which you can communicate at almost any level with your students. You can read the journals daily and read them all if you wish. They truly help you to know about the people you teach. Alice tells the story one journal writing provided, making her appreciate and know more completely her excellent Vietnamese student. The student wrote of her escape from Vietnam. She told about 17 people, including seven in her own family, sailing out of captivity in Communist-controlled Vietnam in a small vessel. They had to construct a false floor in the boat, where all 17 of them lay beneath the floor like sardines in a can. It took them 7 days with minimal food, water, and movement to escape. Alice recalled, years later, how she wept reading the journal and how her humility at being born an American citizen was rekindled every time she thought of that student journal (Wyatt, 1990).

LET STUDENTS KNOW
THEY CAN SUCCEED

Nothing makes you a more successful, effective teacher than having your students succeed. One of the best esteem builders that students can have is the knowledge that their teacher wants to help them succeed. The teacher's attitude can instill in the students a will to do well to please the teacher who cares about them. If you can help them keep that positive attitude foremost in their minds, they will usually rise to your expectations. So, the basic message is, if you plan well and if you feel secure in your material, your students will know that they can do as you have planned and meet your expectations.

You will most likely not have a 100% success rate, and an occasional student will fall through the cracks, as the saying goes, but you can rest well knowing that your students are important enough to you that you will try not to let that happen. If your students know that they are extremely important to you, more important than imparting knowledge or enforcing rules, they will know that they are special. They will be the winners. That winning will be a lifelong lesson and will continue to let you know how effective you have been for years. If teachers do establish that trust, they don't have to worry much about their rules being broken. If students trust their teacher, rarely does that teacher have a problem in getting across the points of the lesson the students need to hear. They want to accomplish to please their teacher, and eventually, to please themselves with an increased self-esteem.

In a recent letter, a student Bob had taught nearly 30 years ago wrote,

> The most important thing I learned in your class was that I could think for myself and that my ideas didn't have to parrot some authority or some textbook. I felt so good about myself when I drew that cartoon when we were working on puns, and I got an "A." I hope you remember. The word I illustrated was "bum steer," and I drew a picture of a big, unshaven, bummy-looking, disheveled, long-horned, bull-like bovine carrying a whiskey bottle and smoking a stub of a cigarette, standing dressed like a bum on Skid Row. I felt such pride as I labeled my drawing "Bum Steer." You showed my pun and

drawing to the class and said how good it was. I had not been recognized before. No one had ever taken the time to say that I was good at anything.

That student went on to become an engineer and made many drawings that helped him become a very wealthy man. His note brought Bob some special pride and partial ownership in that student's success. There are others, too. You will collect such stories for yourself as you accumulate years of experience, and they will be treasures for you to share with others who are new or struggling in the teaching profession.

JOURNAL TOPICS

- What seems to be a valuable lesson about maintaining trust between you and your students?
- How do you see a postmodern approach to teaching and learning working in your classroom?
- If you had a disruptive student with special needs in your classroom, what would you do to aid that student in becoming less disruptive?
- How would you handle the load of reading the writing journals you assign within your classroom?

CHAPTER THREE

Surviving Requires Good Classroom Management

C lassroom management seems to be the monster in first-year teachers' nightmares. Discussions with preservice teachers and first-year teachers reveal that classroom management looms as one of their biggest concerns. Adele, a first-year teacher, tells a story of her fears:

> I will never forget sitting in my secondary methods class one week before I was to begin student teaching. "Dr. Expert," I asked as I tentatively raised my hand, "What do I do if I have discipline problems?" He drew himself up, looked down his nose at me, and said between gritted teeth, "Miss Teacher, if you are a good teacher, you won't *have* discipline problems." Not quite the answer I needed. I entered the student teaching experience filled with dread about the *what if* questions that kept filling my mind.

Fortunately, most of the *what ifs* never developed, and as she acquired experience as a teacher, she learned that classroom management *is* connected to effective instruction and is as much an evolving entity as the profession of teaching.

DESIGNING CLASSROOM MANAGEMENT

Before entering the classroom, you have to develop a plan for dealing with classroom management. However, your *mastery* of classroom management will develop along with your expertise in teaching. It is closely bound to your expectations and your organization of class time. You need to work out rules and consequences that are easy to manage because your main objective is to teach, not referee. Think about behaviors students must exhibit to meet your expectations. For example, if you expect students to complete assignments and come to class prepared, your discipline plan needs to reflect that. If you want to make efficient use of the time you have in class, you will not want students to be tardy or to be milling around the room when the tardy bell rings. That should be reflected in your discipline plan. The following is an excerpt from the English handbook that one teacher prepared for her students each year. Notice how the rules and the explanation of her attendance policy reflect her expectations of the students.

Classroom Rules

1. Be in your seat working by the time the tardy bell stops ringing.
2. Bring paper, pens/pencils, your English notebook, your textbook, and completed assignments to class every day.
3. Keep all objects and body parts to yourself.
4. Use appropriate verbal and body language, and be discreet.
5. Do not steal; this includes stealing a classmate's work by cheating.
6. Follow the teacher's (or substitute's) directions.

Attendance

How can you learn if you are not present? Every day will be an important day in your English education. We do not have "goof off" days or "free" days. It amazes me how many students come back from an absence and ask, "Did we do anything in English?" Excuse me!? Isn't that a rather ridiculous question?

We will always "do something" in English! If you are absent, it is your responsibility to find out what we did and catch up.

Required Attendance

You are required (by law) to be present 90% of the time. That means that on the tenth absence, you have failed. Absences involving participation in school-sponsored activities do not count toward the 90% requirement. There are times when extended absences are granted because of illness. However, there is a paperwork requirement in these cases. Your doctor has to verify the dates and causes of the absences. For example, if you have the flu and miss 4 consecutive days, you may qualify for an extended illness exemption, and those 4 days would be counted as only one absence. Be sure to inform your parents of this because they are the ones who have to work with the school to provide appropriate information and forms.

Tardies

Tardies are punishable by death. . . . Well, not exactly, but they are a serious concern. I want you to be in your seats and already working on your introductory activity by the time the tardy bell starts to ring. Each class period is short enough as it is, so I don't want any time wasted. Therefore, there are two kinds of tardies in our English class:

Out of your seat when the tardy bell stops ringing—You have broken Rule #1, so you get a mark in my grade book, no stamp for the day, and no chance card for the weekly drawing.

Out of the room when the tardy bell stops ringing (even if you are only outside the room for one millisecond after the bell stops)—You have broken Rule #1 as well as a school policy. Sounds like cause for beheading to me. However, instead of being beheaded, you will receive a mark in my grade book, no stamp for the day, no chance card for the week, and a detention assignment. Three of these tardies count as one absence, so don't be careless. Since I am only cruel and not heartless, you have one out-of-the-room tardy pardon for the year. After that, no mercy!

As you can see, her rules were well-defined and structured and reflected the teacher's belief that every minute in her class was important. Class time would not be diverted from her goal of providing quality time for instruction and learning. Some teachers would be comfortable with less definition, and others might want even more. The rules this teacher established for her classroom were rules she felt comfortable monitoring.

If your school has adopted a specific discipline plan, you need to follow guidelines the school has already developed. You will focus on matching your personality and instructional approach with the established rules. If, on the other hand, each teacher develops her own discipline plan, you need to talk with other teachers to see what has worked for them. Think about what you want to happen in your classroom each day. Determine what you will not tolerate. Be aware of consequences that punish you as well as the student. Devise a method for documentation, and think of positive ways to make your discipline plan work.

TALK TO OTHER TEACHERS

You will want to start your school year with your goals and expectations in mind. However, as you learn more about the art of teaching, you will certainly want to make changes—some minor and some important. With that in mind, keep yourself open to learning from other teachers. Observe your colleagues. You don't want to model yourself after a teacher who seems to have no classroom management plan. You also don't want to use a teacher who is a harsh dictator as a model. When you think you have found a teacher who has good classroom management skills, talk with him about what he does in his classroom. Ask him to tell you how he developed his plan and what makes it work well for him. Take notes and think about how his method would work with your personality. Matching the discipline plan to your personality is imperative. For example, if you are a very structured person, you might not be comfortable with a classroom management style that allows students to move freely around the room. If you are a relaxed person, you might not feel comfortable with a classroom management style that requires students to stay in their seats for most of the period. Matching your management style with your personality is extremely important because if you are not comfortable enforcing your own program, you will not be consistent, and consistency is one of the major elements in making any kind of discipline or management plan work.

THINK ABOUT WHAT YOU WANT
TO HAPPEN DAILY IN YOUR CLASSROOM

Being organized is one of the key elements in keeping things running smoothly in your classroom. Most discipline problems occur in the few minutes before class starts or the few minutes before class ends. If you fill these times with meaningful activity and teaching, you will avoid many discipline problems. Your students simply will not have time to cause trouble. So, how do you want your class to start? Have a procedure that you follow religiously each day (Wong & Wong, 1991). Students will know what to expect and will settle into a routine that allows you to begin class, check roll, and take care of all the paper work you must complete before you begin teaching. Your procedure may be something like having students write in journals at the beginning of class each day or work a "problem for the day." It may also be as "freely" structured as having an overhead transparency projected on a screen with different instructions for students each day. Class members begin the projected work while you begin taking roll from a seating chart. By using a seating chart, you can check roll in a few seconds without having to interrupt the activity your students have begun. (Of course, you retain the option of changing the seating chart when you think it needs to be changed.) Use every bit of your class time—especially the time allowed for announcements. Students can multitask, and having activities for them to work on during school announcements is preferable to having them sitting talking, ignoring the announcements, and wasting valuable class time.

COLLECT HOMEWORK AT
THE BEGINNING OF CLASS

Another thing to consider is when you will collect homework assignments. The best time is at the beginning of class. If you want students to keep the papers until later in the class period, you will need a system for making sure they don't try to complete the assignments during the first part of class. For example, if you have assigned something for students to write and you plan to use these texts in group discussions at a later point in the class, walk around the room at the beginning of class—during the introductory activity—and, using a highlighter, mark through the text they have written. That way, if a student hasn't completed the assignment, you have a mark indicating how much of the assignment was actually completed outside of class. This gives you justification for giving that student a lower grade because you know how much of the assignment the student didn't complete as homework.

DETERMINE WHAT YOU WILL NOT TOLERATE

As the teacher, you do not have to tolerate any behavior that makes you or another student uncomfortable. Secondary students are especially adept at saying or doing inappropriate things and then making the teacher feel guilty if he doesn't approve of the students' actions. If you don't like something, say so in a quiet, calm manner—preferably as you stand close to the student. If the student tries to argue with you, calmly tell her that you will be glad to discuss the incident after class. That is usually all that needs to be said. If, however, the student becomes belligerent and threatens to disrupt the class, send another student to the principal's office asking that the principal come and escort the disruptive student from the room. Never allow a student to leave the class unless you have notified the office or made previous arrangements with another teacher to send a student to that teacher's room to work. If you make a habit of having students sit out in the hall or sending them to the principal's office unaccompanied, some students will decide that they would rather spend the time outside of class doing nothing rather than sit inside class participating in class activities. Others will take advantage of being unsupervised and leave the building, putting you at risk because you are responsible for their behavior during the time they are assigned to you. Make it clear to your students that class time is important by keeping students in class if at all possible.

What if you just aren't sure of how to handle a student or a situation? It is fine for you to do nothing more dramatic than to tell a student that you disapprove of her behavior and that you will talk to her after class. If, at the end of class, you still haven't decided on an appropriate way to handle the situation, tell the student that you need to think about what happened in class and decide what you want to do about it. Tell her that you will discuss it with her the next day. That extra time gives you an opportunity to talk with another teacher or your principal, and sometimes to even call the student's parents, and determine a course of action that will be fair and beneficial for the student.

As Susan walked beside a group of students, she heard, "I think Ms. Nelson is a cow!" Susan knew she had heard the comment, and she recognized the voice of one of her antagonistic students. She also knew that this student was adept at confusing any issue of discipline. Without creating any visible disturbance, Susan bent close to the young woman. "Natasha," she whispered, "I want to speak with you after class."

"What?" Natasha said loudly.

Susan put her finger to her lips indicating *do not speak* and began to walk to the next group.

"Ms. Nelson," Natasha called.

"After class," Susan said quietly and continued walking. She didn't know what Natasha would do, but she was hoping her calm approach to the situation would diffuse Natasha's anger. By approaching Natasha quietly and acknowledging the situation without bringing notice to her, Susan had denied the student a forum for rebuttal.

Students don't enjoy staying after class, mainly because it interferes with the social life of the hallway. At the end of class, Natasha headed for the door. "Not so fast, Natasha," Susan called. "We need to talk.

"I didn't do nothin'," Natasha insisted.

"Well, someone in your group called me a *cow*, and I'm pretty sure it was you."

"Not me! You're just pickin' on me!"

Because Susan had allowed herself the rest of the class time to anticipate Natasha's reaction, she had a response ready.

"Let's do this then," she said calmly. "Starting tomorrow, I'm going to move you to another group. That way, when I walk by the group you're with today, I won't falsely accuse you if I hear it again. Because if I hear anything like that again, I'll send the offender to detention and notify the principal about the situation." Now the problem was Natasha's.

"Let me stay, Ms. Nelson. I don't like anyone else in this class."

"Okay, we'll try it, but you know what I expect."

Not all problems are solved so easily, but quite often, giving yourself time to think about the situation will allow you an opportunity to consider all aspects of the problem and to come up with a solution or consequence that is appropriate rather than something that is merely a reaction.

BE AWARE OF CONSEQUENCES PUNISHING YOU AS WELL AS THE STUDENT

How many times have you heard a teacher assign a 500-word essay as punishment? The person most punished is the conscientious teacher who takes the essay and reads and counts each word, or the English teacher who is supposed to teach students to *enjoy* writing. If you must be punitive, there are better ways to enforce your rules. For example, most teachers have to report for duty at least 15 minutes before school starts each morning and stay 15 minutes after school dismisses each day. That provides 30 minutes you can use to require students to stay in your own detention as a consequence of their inappropriate actions. While they are in your room, you may require them to do homework, read books, or do work for you— things like scraping gum off the bottoms of desks, washing off chalkboards, or stapling together papers for the next day's classes. These are things that are easy to supervise, yet they do not cause more work for the teacher. Make sure you have something for students to do. You do not want your punishment to become a time for socializing, either with you or with other students.

IS DETENTION AN OPTION?

Some schools already have consequences built into their program. You may have the option of assigning before-school or after-school detention. There may be a detention available during the lunch period. You may be able to arrange a time-out room with another teacher—a place where you can send a disruptive student so that she is out of your class but still under the supervision of another teacher. Find out what is available to you and then use those options with discretion. The more you are able to handle discipline on your own, the more seriously the principal or vice-principal will take your requests for help. Teachers who send students to the office frequently or without substantial reason will find that they lose the respect of their students and the administrators.

TALK WITH PARENTS

Don't be afraid to call and ask parents for help with your classroom management plan. Calling parents to request their help in dealing with their children can have very positive effects. Keep in mind that you need the parents' cooperation as much as you need the students' cooperation. Many times just calling the parents of one or two difficult students has resulted in the entire class changing unpleasant behavior because they know you do not hesitate to call parents. You will find a more thorough discussion on working with parents in Chapter 7.

DON'T TAKE BEHAVIOR PROBLEMS PERSONALLY

Teachers must develop an ability to detach themselves from disciplinary issues. One thing a teacher must learn is not to take students' behavior personally. Of course, a teacher is generally the target for whatever disruption occurs, but if she refuses to become personally involved, the situation is often easily defused. She must learn to put the offense back on the shoulders of the student. A student who marks up a textbook hasn't marked the teacher's textbook, she has marred the *other students'* textbook. She has to erase or replace the book so that other students can have a textbook. If a student is disruptive in class, he has not irritated just the teacher, he has disturbed the other learners in the classroom. If a student fails to complete a homework assignment, she is damaging *her* grade, not the teacher's. By stepping outside the realm of taking everything personally, it is easier for the teacher to be objective when dealing with unruly or insensitive students.

DEVISE A METHOD FOR DOCUMENTATION

The first step in planning for documentation is to create a folder for each student and file the folders close to your desk in a secured file cabinet. Use the folders to keep artifacts and information about your students that you might need in a student or parent conference. Early in the year you should ask students to write a short text for you. It could be a paragraph, a letter, or a short essay. You want it to be something that shows the student's style of writing and his handwriting. This will be your reference if you suspect that the student is having someone else do his homework. Although many students now have access to computers and no longer turn in handwritten homework, you will still have a piece that you can use to determine if the style of the writing matches that of the sample paper you collected.

The individual student folders are also good places to file exceptional work that you want to share with parents or display (with the student's permission) in the classroom. You may also use the folders to file tests that you don't want the students to keep or that you want to return at a later time so students may use them for study guides.

Finally, the folders will give you a place to keep tardy slips, used passes, notes students try to pass during class, and any other bits of information that might be useful to you in parent conferences. Anecdotal records may also be stored in the folders. For example, if a student caused trouble in a class or became belligerent or obnoxious, at the end of class (and sometimes at the time of the incident), the teacher could jot down a brief description of the incident on a notepad and drop the description into that student's folder. At the end of the day, the teacher should retrieve the note and type a brief description of the incident. She must be careful to be honest. For example, if she raised her voice to the student or did something she later felt was inappropriate, she should put that into the account also. With her efforts to be honest about her responses, she increases her credibility if she has to visit with the principal or parents about the student.

FURTHER RECORD KEEPING

Keeping a record of student misconduct should also be part of the teacher's grade book. Listing classroom rules and numbering them gives you a handy code to use in documentation. If, for instance, a student throws a pencil across the room, that would fall under the third rule in the rules listed below.

Classroom Rules

1. Be in your seat working by the time the tardy bell stops ringing.
2. Bring paper, pens and pencils, your English notebook, your textbook, and completed assignments to class every day.
3. Keep all objects and body parts to yourself.
4. Use appropriate verbal and body language, and be discreet.
5. Do not steal; this includes stealing a classmate's work by cheating.
6. Follow the teacher's (or substitute's) directions.

If no one was injured, you simply remark that the student has broken Rule #3, and write "#3" on the student's record in the grade book (or on a notepad you carry with you). If a student fails to turn in homework, you record #2 in the grade book. By doing this, the student and teacher can readily see if a pattern of behavior is developing and take measures to correct the behavior.

BE AWARE OF CONFIDENTIALITY REQUIREMENTS

A federal law you must know and understand is the Family Education Rights and Privacy Act—the confidentiality law (Orlich, Harder, Callahan, & Gibson, 2001). This law is broken so often out of ignorance that it is amazing schools are not in constant litigation because of the actions of their teachers. According to this law, information concerning students is to be kept strictly confidential. The only way information is to be passed from one teacher to the other is in a private area, such as an office, away from other people, especially students. A teacher or administrator should share confidential information only if teachers *need to know* that information in order to be more effective in teaching that particular student. What does that do to gossip? It eliminates it. By nature, teachers want to know as much about their students as possible. Usually this is a good trait. If they know what is happening to a student outside the classroom, it is easier for them to adjust instructions or tolerate behavior inside the classroom when it results from problems students are experiencing. The problem for educators comes when teachers cross from sharing information in order to help a student to sharing information because it is interesting. Make it a practice from the very beginning of your career to discuss students only in the privacy of a closed office and only if the information discussed is crucial to your working with a particular student.

HOW TO HANDLE PUBLICIZED GRADES

With more schools using computer programs to record and store grades, there is less likelihood of students' grades being publicized. In reality, however, there are many school districts that don't have such technology available for their teachers. In those cases, teachers must be careful not to breech confidentiality laws.

In one school without computer grading systems, the principal's secretary compiled a list each week indicating which students were on academic probation and which ones were ineligible to participate in school activities. This was done in response to the state's "No Pass, No Play" requirement. In order to keep her students informed, each Friday when the list was given to the teachers, Tina took sticky notes and wrote the name of each student from her classes who appeared on that list and the class or classes each was failing. Then after she checked the roll, and while students were writing in their journals, she went around the room giving the information quietly to each student on the list. Tina's faculty had not been instructed on how to notify students, and she frequently had students tell of seeing another student's name on the probation/ineligibility list when the list was passed around in another teacher's classroom. Some teachers read the list aloud to each class as a means of notifying students. Some posted the list on the bulletin board. All of these methods breached the confidentiality law, and if challenged by a student or parent, the school administrators could not have defended those teachers.

SHOULD STUDENTS MARK
EACH OTHER'S PAPERS?

Another common practice is to have students grade each other's papers (or maybe grade their own papers) and then call out grades while the teacher records them in the grade book. This practice was challenged by parents in an Oklahoma community (Simpson, 2000). Although the courts found in favor of the school, this accentuates the issue of treating students with compassion. Students at each end of the grading spectrum are often harassed when a teacher follows this practice. Those who consistently make the higher grades are subject to teasing, and those who consistently make the lower grades may be humiliated. It's true that it takes a teacher longer to record grades going through the papers individually; however, it is better for a teacher to take the extra time than to be guilty of embarrassing students.

Teachers compromise matters of confidentiality if they allow students to see other students' grades for any reason. For example, if a student comes to the teacher and wants to check his grade, the teacher should keep the open grade book from the student's view or cover the grades and names of the other students when showing a specific grade. Again, think how you would feel if your grades were poor and your peers were allowed to see what you had made and compare it to their own grades. As always, by putting yourself in the shoes of those you teach, you are more likely to treat students fairly and compassionately.

POSITIVE WAYS TO MAKE YOUR
CLASSROOM MANAGEMENT PLAN WORK

The best thing you can do to make your classroom management plan work is to be consistent. If you work hard to enforce your plan faithfully, students will appreciate your efforts and even join with you in your consistency. They will remind you if you fail to enforce your plan. It is important for you to develop an attitude of openness to students' pointing out errors and inconsistencies they see in your administration of the classroom rules. Don't become defensive. Instead, thank the students for correcting your error and then enforce the rule. This may seem almost cruel if the student who has broken the rule is one of your very best students and one who never causes trouble. However, if you play favorites, your students will resent you *and* the student who receives the exception to the rule.

REWARDING GOOD BEHAVIOR

So many times, students who follow the rules and work hard are often ignored in classes, especially if the class as a whole is rowdy or apathetic. Early in John's career, he looked for a way to reward good behavior. The plan that seemed to work best for him was the assertive discipline model developed by Canter (Canter & Canter, 1976). Canter's plan seemed to be effective at the elementary level but lacking at the secondary level. However, John was so intent on finding a way to reward good behavior that he worked with Canter's material to make it suitable for the students he taught. Even years later, when assertive discipline was no longer in vogue, John's plan still worked with his students. What he realized, however, was that his students' desire to work hard and behave well was in no way affected by the rewards he gave. Working hard and behaving well are intrinsically motivated (Ornstein, 1990). No student would turn in her work and follow John's class rules so that she would receive a stamp at the end of class or a piece of candy at the end of the week. What his brand of assertive discipline did was give him a way to say "thank you" to students who had done what he'd asked them to do, a way to reward "good" students who are so often ignored.

In the spirit of good humor, at the end of the week, any student who was present 3 days out of the week and had broken no rules was given a chance card (or ticket) that was put into a box for a weekly drawing. One student in each class received a candy bar. Again, this was not anything that motivated students to refrain from breaking rules. Instead, it was a way to reward students who had done what they were supposed to do. John was always amazed at the excitement the weekly drawing generated for high school students. His students never let him forget the Friday drawing, and they good-naturedly monitored the awarding of tickets—"Hey, Julie missed 3 days this week!" "Tom came in late today!" An additional benefit to this drawing was that it also served as a reminder to students who were tardy or had failed to turn in work.

ENCOURAGING SELF-DISCIPLINE

One of the most difficult tasks for a teacher (and also one of the most important) is encouraging students to develop self-discipline. Students come to your class from varied backgrounds of responsibility and self-indulgence. The best way to encourage them to develop self-discipline is to be consistent in what you require. You must be the role model for all of your students. You cannot insist that they turn in work on time if you show up for classes unprepared. You cannot insist that they follow your rules if you show partiality to some students or haphazardly enforce the rules you have established. You cannot insist that they treat each other with respect if you do not treat students and colleagues with respect. The way a successful teacher encourages self-discipline among his students is to exhibit self-discipline himself.

Another way to encourage self-discipline is to insist that students treat each other kindly. It is impossible for a teacher to be aware of everything that happens in a classroom. However, a teacher will hear and see *most* of what happens. It is important that you not allow harassment, intimidation, or ridicule from any of your students. Students may not realize that what they are doing is inappropriate. If at all possible, you should speak with offending students privately the first time they act unkindly. Explain why the behavior is inappropriate and why you will not tolerate it in your class. Be prepared for disagreement. The student may be imitating behavior of his family or peers and may truly not realize that he is being offensive. You must remain calm and positive as you discuss the issue, but you must also be prepared to insist that the student stop the behavior, whether he understands your reasoning or not. Again, as in dealing with discipline issues, if you can avoid responding to the student as if you are personally offended, you will be able to remain objective as you explain what is acceptable in your classroom. If the student continues to be offensive, then you need to take more assertive action and see that the behavior stops. You might want to enlist the help of the school counselor to determine ways to work with students who don't seem to understand the need to be tolerant of their classmates.

All successful teachers have had to learn classroom management. All of us have made mistakes and wished we could have handled some things differently. Because we want to be good teachers, we often worry unnecessarily about how we are working with students. Remember our advice to be kind to yourself. Secondary students are perceptive. They see the heart of a teacher regardless of the mask the teacher may wear. The old adage "actions speak louder than words" is especially true for young people. An effective teacher truly cares for his students. He wants to teach them all that he can, and he wants his students to learn. Even when students are challenging and inequities in the system are obvious, an effective teacher sees the best in his students and the best in the educational system. Because she cares, her students will care, and together they will reach, and exceed, their expectations.

DEALING WITH
POSSIBLE VIOLENCE

For the most part, school is a safe place. Sadly, however, school personnel must be aware of potential danger. All schools are required to have policies in place for dealing with crises. Ask for this policy, read it carefully, jot down any questions you have about the procedure, and walk through the procedure yourself.

Examine your surroundings carefully to see if there are potentially dangerous areas. For example, are there places outside your classroom door where someone could hide or where weapons or explosives could be stored? Are there things along designated escape routes that might fall on students or block their path?

Thinking about a violent incident occurring can be frightening and very unsettling. However, if you have a plan for dealing with such an incident and know it well, you and your students can relax and get on with the business of learning. Elaine watched a very caring middle school teacher prepare her students for emergency situations. The school was located near a large metropolitan area where a bombing had occurred, and school safety was a looming concern for parents, teachers, and administrators. The teacher in this middle school classroom walked around the room, talking to the children in a calm voice. She told them that if they heard something that sounded like gunshots being fired or if the principal interrupted class to announce a crisis situation, they were to very quietly get under their desks. "Let's practice that now," she said.

The students quickly did as she instructed. "Good! You were so quiet," she encouraged. "Now get back into your chairs, and let me tell you what I would do." The children quietly returned to their seats and listened. "I would hurry to the door, lock it, turn out the lights, and then crouch behind my desk." She did these things as she talked. "Now," she said as she stood smiling in front of the room again, "One thing you need to remember. I will never leave you in here alone. I will always stay with you and take care of you."

Once the teacher had finished her instructions and practice, she continued with her social studies lesson for the day. Students took books out of their desks, turned to the page she instructed, and began their lesson. Her calm manner and her reassurance that she would take care of the students took away the tension and fear that could have grown from such a presentation.

Although practicing an emergency procedure worked well for the teacher mentioned above, your district might not condone such an exercise. The administrators and school board may fear that by practicing a procedure, the teacher might be creating a stressful situation for her students. Ask your principal about the need for practicing classroom procedures for emergency situations. If she says that would not be appropriate, you must follow her lead and refrain from planning such an activity. That doesn't mean, however, that you should ignore the issue. For your own preparation, think through what you might do if your students were threatened. Don't share the information with your students, but have a plan of action and practice it mentally so that, if you are faced with a violent or threatening situation, you will be mentally and emotionally prepared to do what is necessary and best for your students.

FOCUSING ON RESPECT

In working with preservice teachers, we often hear them talk about wanting their students to respect them. In the area of classroom management, respect is certainly a reciprocal agreement. Students will always remember teachers who humiliate them, and those memories will be filled with anger and resentment. Students will also remember teachers who treated them with respect. In dealing with your students, try to remember those times when a teacher embarrassed you. Try to keep that from happening to your students. It is possible to be firm and authoritative without being rude. Speaking to your students calmly and quietly, asking them to stay after class to discuss disagreements or outbursts, planning for a place where they can go to cool off are all strategies that help diffuse their emotion and anger. Letting them know that you want to help them save face with their peers will make them more willing to listen to what you have to say and give them the option of cooperation.

JOURNAL TOPICS

- What kinds of behavior do you want to encourage in your students? What are some ideas of ways to encourage that behavior?
- What are some behaviors that you will not tolerate in your classroom? How could you respond to students who were engaging in those behaviors?
- What are some effective classroom management techniques you have seen other teachers use?

CHAPTER FOUR

Surviving Includes Good Lesson Plans

O ne of the most productive tools that you will use in your teaching career is the lesson plan. There are many different kinds of lesson plans, and often schools have their own format to follow when preparing lessons. Whatever the design style, a good lesson plan is your friend. Very often, seasoned teachers will say to you something like, "I don't know why they teach you all that business about lesson plans in your education classes at the college. You'll never have the time to design that kind of plan." But following the precepts of this chapter will make your life as a teacher much easier and much more rewarding. And, although creating lesson plans is hard work, a well-planned lesson not only helps you teach the material that you want to cover but also helps you fill the class period with meaningful activity—a necessary ingredient for good classroom management. Although there will certainly be times when what you have planned does not work as you had hoped, if you plan activities that involve students, they will get the benefit of what they themselves work out. One excellent benefit of making the thorough lesson plan is that you can put the plan in a notebook to use again and again. If the plans are good, they will allow reuse with little effort to you. Your students will never realize when a lesson is recycled.

CREATING A MASTER PLAN

The very first thing you should do is to fill in your plan book for one semester. That means that you check your calendar against the official school calendar and plot in all of the holidays, parent-teacher conference days, testing dates, and so forth. You may be amazed at how few days are left to accomplish your teaching goals, but you need to know where and when the interruptions occur. Next, mark the end of grading periods, scheduled semester exams, and dates for sending out grade reports, deficiency notices, and any other kinds of notices that might be required by your district. After these dates and times are marked on your planning calendar, you are ready to think about what you want to cover in your classes. This fact alone causes some stress for teachers. They will readily think, "I came here to teach, and we are going to spend so many days or hours out of the classroom, how will I ever get everything done!" This is a legitimate complaint, but when something is beyond your control—and administrative chores are—then you just have to go along with the time out of class and plan accordingly.

Of course, you have checked the standards for your subject area. These standards are the goals set by your state department of education or the national standards from your professional organization, such as Standards for the English Language Arts set by the National Council for Teachers of English, National Science Education Standards set by the National Research Council, National Standards for History set by the National Council for History in the Schools, and Curriculum and Evaluations Standards for School Mathematics set by the National Council of Teachers of Mathematics. There are many others, in areas such as science, foreign language, reading, the arts, health, history, civics, economics, geography, physical education, and social studies (Marzano & Kendall, 2006). Each has a set of standards that should be used along with your state's standards to help you plan your teaching. You also need a copy of the school's curriculum guide. In schools where such a guide is not available, your textbook may be the best source of basic curriculum outline (its table of contents may be a guide for you to follow) as you use it hand in hand with the national and state standards. You will certainly want to know the basic precepts of the No Child Left Behind Act so

that you can make your lesson plans meet the needs of tests generated to keep the students equal. You need some sort of guideline so
that you will know what you are expected to teach. Most of these
standards are available on professional Web sites.

As you start to think about and plan your academic year, you
will discover there is no way to cover everything you would like
to teach. Using the standards as a guide, prioritize. Some things
students must know in order to build on the subject matter or to
pass mandated exams. You are the highly qualified teacher who is
responsible to assure that all of your students know the material
for these exams and can pass the exams. There are other things
beyond the standards that you would be pleased if your students
would learn. Finally, there are things you love about your subject
area that could really be omitted. Identifying these "not truly necessary" areas is a painful task. It's difficult to imagine others not
wanting to know all you have learned about your subject matter
in your specialized classes. You must try, however, to focus on
what will make a difference to your students after they have left
your class. These are the lessons you must concentrate on first.
If time allows and the students are very interested, then adding
those other items of learning will work. If all your requirements
are met and students can pass the exams on those areas, then
bring in that special book, that favorite experiment, and those
wonderful mind bogglers that promote critical thinking.

One of the easiest ways to organize what you will teach is by
isolating and defining major units of study as you plan your curriculum. Then you can break those units into weeks and days.
This is where you must consult your master calendar. You need to
organize your units so that they end in time for you to compute
and report grades for specific grading periods. You also need to
organize in such a way that due dates for assignments are realistic, aware that you will have to be constantly adjusting to compen-
sate for changes in the school's daily schedules and to allow you
time to re-teach material when your students haven't progressed
as well as you had hoped. Although excellent organization is reassuring to you, as a teacher, you must remember to be flexible.
Allow yourself time to reengage the students in the same material
for additional class periods if necessary. Two important things to
remember are to protect your holiday and break time and, fur-
thermore, not to make major assignments due on the day before a

break. You, the teacher, need a break just as much as your students. Don't make the mistake of planning due dates so that your break is filled with grading those assignments or with dreading not having them graded when the break is over. Remember that it is good to give graded papers back to the students as quickly as you can do so. The immediacy of review comes right at that moment when they are most ready to correct mistakes in their thinking if they have fallen short of the goal.

WRITING LESSON OBJECTIVES

Once you have decided what you want to teach, determine what your students should learn from the material you want to cover. This means that you must write objectives. Objectives (or learner outcomes) are essential for the teacher if there is to be some kind of a framework in which learners learn. Objectives lead the teacher to identify the skills and material they want their students to learn by the time the lesson is ended. They establish some kind of criteria on which the assessments of the lesson hinge. Once you begin thinking about what your students are doing and learning, you will discover that within one lesson you could write at least a dozen objectives. That, however, would make your planning unwieldy. Instead, you might prefer to differentiate the objectives to meet the needs of the various students within your classroom. Identifying three or four objectives that you will directly address for each day's lesson is preferable to setting many objectives that are poorly covered. This is another example of when "less is more" is a valuable adage.

One thing that you should think about, though it is an objectionable truth, is that often your students' thinking will be in short spurts. This is very likely due to the way they have grown up watching television. They get commercial breaks very often during a television show, and their minds can't be stimulated easily for long periods without such breaks. It may be better to have objectives that can be met in 10 minutes or so, or to break the segments of an objective to those shorter periods so that you have a good start to keep students interested. It is disagreeable to think that teachers have to think of themselves as a form of entertainment, but this is a reflection of our society, and if you teach adults who are not part of a captive group, they will respond the same way as your young students.

Wong and Wong (1991) suggest that teachers let the students know precisely what is expected and keep that intent before them during the entire class period. They suggest that the best way to keep it foremost in the students' minds is for the teacher to write the objective for that day's class on the upper left-hand corner of the chalkboard or some other especially designated space in the room. Students know, from that objective's prominence in the classroom, exactly what they are expected to achieve for that class period. You may not want to display your objectives for the students. It may work better for you to tell students, "Today we are going to . . ." or "Our objective for today is. . . ." Do what works best for you, but use some kind of signaling to direct your students' attention to the desired results of the class to prepare them for the plan for the day. If they know what is expected of them, they will at least come closer to achieving that goal. The objective may have to be verbally repeated several times during a class period to reiterate what you expect. A teacher can ask, "What is our objective in this first part of the lesson, class?" If she gets no answer, then there may be a need to re-teach some material.

An example of this is when I came into my pedagogy class and wrote up on the corner of the board as Wong and Wong (1991) suggested: "Our objective for the first part of the period will be to find out some details about shapes and the use of a protractor to discover truths." I gave each group of four a paper with a set of shapes: two triangles, one rectangle, a trapezoid, a pentagon, and an octagon. I gave each group a protractor. I said, "I will give you 8 minutes to consider the shapes and do whatever you can with them and the protractor to determine some facts that you can report back to the class. This is discussion time, so work together to determine some currently unknown facts." Most were not math majors. Few remembered what to do with the protractor. One said, "I don't remember what to do with a protractor, but I do remember that it is used to measure angles."

My response was, "That is a fact that you may put into your list. I don't want to tell you any more than that, but perhaps when the four of you work together you can discover what to do to the angles of those shapes." After a series of other questions fielded in my direction, we had some other facts that were emerging. I reiterated the objective, "Write several facts that you discovered with the use of the shapes and the protractor. Since we are running short of time from the original 8 minutes, I will give you 8 more minutes." I could see their frustration, but also the fact that they were learning by working together, putting little bits of knowledge into play.

At the conclusion of the second 8 minutes, I asked them to report what they had learned. Most gave mundane facts: A pentagon has five angles and five straight sides; an octagon has eight angles and eight sides; the protractor is used to measure angles. Then one group said, "We discovered that if you measure the angles in the two triangles, the three angles together equal 180 degrees. That means that every three angled shape has 180 degrees. Every four-angled item then has 360 degrees." I congratulated them and asked them to use their clear protractor on a transparency I had of the triangles and the quadrilateral shapes and show how to measure. Then I asked each group to do that with their shapes. It was amazing how they got "into" that lesson about a subject that hardly anyone cared about in that particular classroom. I looked at the clock and said, "We have only 2 minutes until the class ends. Who can state the objective for today?" (It was stated), then "How do we know that we reached that objective." They answered.

The class was a great success. It showed planning, but it also showed flexibility and once more restates the idea of differentiation being done by grouping and sharing. They achieved my goal of understanding a pedagogical technique to get them thinking.

Another reason for identifying and stating your objectives is that it will help you make sure that you are matching your instruction with criteria established by your district and state. By taking the time to indicate how your objectives move your students toward addressing mandated standards, you are not only doing what your school or state requires, you are reassuring yourself that you are providing meaningful instruction that will help your students learn the established curriculum. If "passing the test" is very important in your community and your state, you will also reassure yourself that you are getting the students ready for their upcoming exams. You will have also done your part in giving your students equal instruction for No Child Left Behind.

As a review, you need to compose both goals and objectives. Goals are broadly worded guidelines and are helpful in planning a unit of study. For example, in teaching *Macbeth*, one goal might be for students to understand Shakespeare's development of character. Objectives would be specific things the students would do as they worked toward that goal. An objective might state: Students will identify dynamic characters in Act I and explain why they are dynamic and not static.

BLOOM'S TAXONOMY

In the mid-1950s, Benjamin Bloom (Bloom, Englehart, Furst, Hill, & Krathwohl, 1956) published a book introducing his three domains of learning: thought (Cognitive), emotion (Affective), and physicality (Psychomotor). Each of the domains is set up in a hierarchical taxonomy of learning. Each progressive level of learning relies on the accomplishment of a previous level of learning. If the teacher has Bloom's Learning Taxonomy in mind, she can use verbs designated for each level and can tell from reading the objective at just what level the learner is expected to achieve. Mager (1984) also suggests that if a teacher knows her students and their capability level and style of learning, she can set up objectives that every member of a given class may attain. It is true that special planning would have to be done to keep more than one level of learning going at one time in a classroom, but if the teacher is a facilitator instead of a dispenser of knowledge, she can accomplish this feat. Also keep in mind that you do not address all of these domains in one lesson. From a practical standpoint, you need to select material to teach, divide the material into lessons, write objectives for each lesson, and plan your instruction. If you find that you have neglected one or more of the domains and mandated outcomes you needed to address, then you know you need to rethink and redirect your lessons.

Cognitive Domain: Knowledge Level

Bloom divides the cognitive domain into six progressive levels. The first three of the six are at the concrete learning stages. The first level of the cognitive domain is the *knowledge* level. This level designates a time for the student to use simple recall or recognition of materials. Specific verbs for this level would include verbs such as *list, identify, locate, recognize, match, state, label, describe,* and *name.* If the teacher wanted to write an objective at this level, it would read something like this: "At the end of today's lesson, the student will list the thirteen original colonies and will describe their climates and environments." For the most part, this is an easy lesson to learn. This level lays the foundation for all the thinking that occurs for the learner. At this stage, the learner is gathering a great deal of data that can be useful later to enhance the topic about which the facts have been gathered.

Cognitive Domain: Comprehension Level

The second level of the cognitive domain is the *comprehension* level. This stage is the first level of understanding, albeit a nominal understanding, of a given topic. Whereas the first level is generally not much more than memorization or recitation of given facts, it requires some rudimentary understanding. Verbs that introduce objectives pertinent to this level of learning are *paraphrase, define, illustrate, restate, describe, rewrite, summarize, distinguish, infer, explain, generalize,* and *translate.* An objective at this level could be stated something like this: "At the end of today's lesson, students will explain the differences in attitude of the American patriots of the American Revolution and the English sympathizers of that time period." This is the place where the student of American history would be able to state her opinions about what was happening in colonial times in America. She would also be able to tell how she would know the differences among the people who were English settlers and their competing visions for the future of the colonies.

Cognitive Domain: Application Level

The *application* level is the stage of learning when the student is able to put to use the material he has learned up to this point. This is the pre-abstract thinking stage when students are first asked to solve problems. They can make generalizations based on the information they have memorized and to which they have been able to put some meaning.

Some verbs that readily introduce this stage of the cognitive domain are *use, adapt, discover, gather, modify, survey, graph, solve, show, compute, determine, operate,* and *prepare.* An objective at this level could be stated in this manner: "At the end of today's lesson, students will solve a problem showing the congruent angles between a parallelogram and a house roof, given the measurements of the parallelogram and the measurements of the longer sides of the house roof." The student can determine, from identification of like angles and the formulas that she has been given for parallelograms, the measurement of the two shorter sides of a roof, citing a real-world (authentic) problem she might confront.

Cognitive Domain: Analysis Level

The fourth level is the *analysis* level. This is the first truly abstract thinking level of the cognitive domain of learning. The idea of the analysis level is for the learner to break down all the information given into some kind of workable categories or parts so that it can be more easily or more comprehensibly explained. This analysis level takes some item of knowledge and moves it from its more complex to its more basic, simpler parts. To help you distinguish this level from others in writing objectives, use words such as *select, discriminate, determine, distinguish, separate, differentiate, infer, relate, divide, break down, classify, categorize, compare,* and *analyze.* An example of an analysis-level objective might be, "At the end of the lesson, students will categorize each word in the sentence into its separate part of speech." Students will be responsible, then, for knowing and defining the parts of speech and applying the rules for each so that the words in given sentences can be categorized into the various parts of speech, according to usage in the sentence.

Cognitive Domain: Synthesis Level

The fifth level of the cognitive domain is the *synthesis* level. At this level, the student can take apart analyzed elements and put them back together again, creating some kind of a new whole by such reassembly. It should be noted specifically that a new, unique form must be produced with the available sources. Verbs that would designate this level of learning in writing objectives would be *design, compile, compose, combine, invent, develop, conclude, construct, devise, incorporate, integrate, depict, produce, plan,* and *organize.* At this level, students will have gone through the four previous levels with an understanding that they will take the pieces of information they have identified, explained, used, and broken down into varied parts, and create something new from all that learning. An example objective for this level might be, "At the end of today's lesson, students will take a group of brainstormed adjectives and participles, verbs, nouns, and pronouns and combine them in such a way as to write a diamante formula poem."

Cognitive Domain: Evaluation Level

The sixth level of the cognitive domain is the *evaluation* level. This stage requires that students take all the information they possess up to this point and make some kind of a judgment based on the material they have collected. Students must make a value judgment as to the pertinence of the material or the ideas that they have gained from the other levels of learning. Some verbs that would help to show that process would be *justify, critique, decide, judge, recommend, interpret, evaluate,* and *appraise.* This is a very high level of learning and does require the students to muster a great deal of gathered data, discussion, and understanding. An example of an objective written for this level could be, "At the end of today's lesson students will justify the actions of Captain Ahab as he risks the lives of his sailors for the final onslaught of Moby-Dick." Students cannot just jot something down off the tops of their heads. They have to cite references from other authors and critics, cite materials all through *Moby-Dick,* or do more than just describe "gut" feelings if they are to "justify." This level requires the student to have developed a great deal of knowledge and ability in order to complete the process. It is a worthy goal for the culmination of some studies.

Affective Domain

The affective domain has five levels of learning. The objectives relating to this domain are generally concerned with the attitudes and emotions of students. Some argue that this domain is more appropriately relegated to the church and the home, and that is, to some extent, a warranted observation. There are times, however, when affective domain learning can be assigned to the classroom. Measurable objectives are difficult to write in this domain because it is difficult for a teacher to evaluate how much a student's attitude or emotions are involved. There must be some kind of choice available for the student for the affective domain to be useful in a school situation. Students must be able to make a choice and not have to bend to the will of a teacher or a peer about the judgments they make or the choices they choose to follow. Krathwohl, Bloom, and Masia (1964) have developed five stages a person goes through in learning to establish attitudes or values. It is important that you have these at your disposal if you are doing an affective domain lesson. The five stages of the affective domain are called *receiving level, responding level, valuing level, organization level,* and *characterization by a value* or *a value complex level.* Each level deals with the degree of internalization of a specific value, attitude, or emotion approached by the student.

Very often, drama teachers, speech teachers, debate teachers, English teachers (literature particularly), art teachers, and music teachers are looking to the affective domain to guide them. Objectives may be written to express some degree of observable measurement, and verbs indicating the various levels will help the teacher to see that a hierarchy does exist and that until a student realizes one level of involvement, she cannot be taught at a higher plane.

Psychomotor Domain

The final domain that Bloom identified is the *psychomotor domain.* This domain is especially relevant to physical education, music, art, and the various vocational educations such as agriculture, business, or home economics. The taxonomy was the last to be developed and implemented. There are many interpretations of this domain, but the interpretation we have chosen to share is developed by Harrow (1972). He has delineated four levels of learning in this domain. The four levels are *fundamental movement* (little control by participant), *generic movement* (basic movement), *ordinative movement* (some control and improvisation), and *creative movement* (movement unique to the student). There is still a hierarchical order for this domain, and the student cannot be expected to complete the third level, for instance, until the first and second levels have been completed.

BLOOM EXPLAINED WITH
A NEW PERSPECTIVE

Marzano and Kendall (2006) have looked carefully at Bloom's Taxonomy and have expanded his taxonomy in a new book, *The New Taxonomy of Educational Objectives*. This new look is a valuable tool for a complete use of Bloom in this new age of learning. They have four levels that encompass all three of the domains in three-dimensional thought. Their four levels are retrieval, comprehension, analysis, and knowledge utilization. They are simplistically stated here so that they can generate a new interest in Bloom and so you can further encapsulate your lesson objectives.

Retrieval Level

They divide their retrieval level into the following:

Recognizing, where the student validates correct statements about the topic being studied.

Recalling, where the student produces correct statements about the topic being studied.

Executing, where the student produces the answer to the problem in the topic being studied.

Comprehension Level

In their comprehension level the student

Integrates the newly learned material with what he already knows. He describes how the material fits into the larger picture of knowledge of the topic.

Symbolizes the topic so he can give a graphic representation of the learned new material.

Analysis Level

At the analysis level the student matches this knowledge with other pertinent information.

Knowledge Utilization

This is the point at which the student can use the knowledge, integrated into his own schema to understand the problems of the topic well enough to solve them by himself.

GARDNER'S MULTIPLE INTELLIGENCES

We have to talk for a moment about Gardner's Multiple Intelligences (1993) if we are to have fully developed lesson plans. There is so much information on this topic that we will not opt for more than just a rudimentary discussion, but full discussions can easily be found at several Web sites and also by reading Gardner's books, which are included in the references for this book. Thinking about and incorporating the theory of multiple intelligences into your instruction builds in success for students who don't learn in the more traditional ways.

Gardner has isolated and named nine intelligences. A tenth one is very likely to be added soon as it is somewhat different from the others. He contends that he may find as many as thirty with distinct descriptions. True, you cannot make every lesson address every intelligence, but if you don't address each intelligence some of the time, some of your students will miss out on their high capability levels and will not enter into your lessons as readily as they might. Everyone wants to have his own capability touched at some time to help him more fully get into what is being taught. Using the intelligences in lesson planning will also aid in making the lesson authentic. Planning to use the different intelligences somewhere in your lesson plan will certainly aid you in engaging nearly all of the students at least some of the time, and as they recognize that you are making efforts to involve them, they will respect you more. That respect will then make for a better relationship between you and your students.

The nine intelligences that Gardner has isolated at this time include these: *verbal/linguistic, logical/mathematical, bodily/kinesthetic, visual/spatial, musical/rhythmical, interpersonal, intrapersonal, naturalistic,* and *spiritual/existential.* A new intelligence, *moral,* will perhaps soon be added by Gardner to his list.

Verbal/Linguistic

Words are very important to the students who excel in this intelligence. They love to read, speak, and write. They have an aptitude for word games. They seem to do better in English, social studies, and humanities. They love to study encyclopedias and dictionaries because they love to know word histories and idea histories. They have conversations often and love to discuss or write on a given topic. They are detail-oriented and love to share the details verbally. Listening is a big part of this person's interest, too. If your teaching assignment is one that is generally all psychomotor or affective (such as physical education or art), be sure that you include some time in your class that is dedicated to verbal/linguistic activity. It is very easy to go about your physical activities or your painting or sculpting in the classroom without doing much verbalization. As part of your lessons, you need to give the "verbal/linguistic" students a chance to verbalize.

Logical/Mathematical

Numbers are as important to these kinds of thinkers as words are to the verbal/linguistic thinkers. Mathematics and science are among the favorite subjects for students with this intelligence. A logical person can solve brainteasers. Thought in clear, abstract, wordless, imageless concepts appeals to this type of intelligence, which promotes measurement, categorization, and analysis. Teachers should strive to make lessons that address this kind of thinking because young people live in a technological world that requires logic for its fulfillment.

Visual/Spatial

The students strong in visual/spatial intelligence enjoy using a camera or a camcorder to "picture" learning. They enjoy mazes, puzzles that are visual, and visualizing items that the verbally intelligent describe. They like to draw and doodle. They like to construct and make pictures for others to follow along with stories. They need illustrations or to illustrate. These students need some space in the lesson to illustrate what the lesson teaches.

Bodily/Kinesthetic

The bodily/kinesthetic intelligence requires learners to engage in hands-on, concrete activities such as sewing, carpentry, carving, knitting, or designing a model to build. These students often use a great deal of body language to make a point in their conversation. They need tactile situations. They need to rehearse and practice to make their skills perfect. They are rhythmical, and they like to beat time to the music they hear, even if none is playing.

They might be thought of as being somewhat hyper, but generally, they just learn by movement.

Musical/Rhythmic

The musical/rhythmic learners enjoy music and like to sing or dance. They like to listen to music and can tell when music is played off-key. They learn better in a classroom if there is any kind of music playing in the background. They often hum a tune as they work. Music runs through their heads, and they can take part in many activities if they are allowed to produce some kind of musical background sounds to enhance the piece of literature, art, or even mathematics that they are studying. Teachers can easily add rhythm or music to their classrooms. They will find that students with this intelligence respond to almost any situation with music.

Interpersonal

Those learners with strong interpersonal intelligence like to be with other people and get to know everything about everyone else. They love group activities and social events.

They are the peer teachers of the group because they constantly want to share what they know or have perfected. They just want to be with people and help others solve problems.

Intrapersonal

People strong in this intelligence are always trying to find out how they themselves operate. They have realistic views of strengths and weaknesses. They tend to be rather quiet and reserved, and they need some time alone so they can think. This group will benefit if the lesson includes a time to write personal thoughts or plans in a journal. They are very clear about their goals in life because they have spent time learning about themselves.

Naturalistic

The naturalistically intelligent students associate many ideas with nature and outdoor activities. They are much more at home around animals and plants than they are around other human beings. These learners collect nature objects. They think a great deal about the way that humans take care, or don't take care, of environmental concerns. Teachers need to plan some activities, even in English or mathematics classes, to pull in naturalistic elements. Students with this kind of intelligence should have a chance to show it somewhere besides science or agriculture classrooms. Gardner added naturalistic intelligence to his list in the mid-1990s.

Spiritual/Existential

These thinkers are involved with themselves and their roles in the greater picture of life. They enjoy discussing history and ancient cultures to see where mankind today fits into the larger picture. They try to examine the relationship between humankind and the universe or humankind and God according to their own personal beliefs. They sometimes have the "I am what I am attitude" of an existentialist philosopher, and teachers need to realize that these are very helpful people if their attitudes can be harnessed for classroom use. These students need some discussion time for just talking about life and the universe in general.

Moral

The research into the moral intelligence seems to place it as being something different from the spiritual intelligence. Moral, in this instance, would look at one's relationship with all living things and their well-being. Morality is often dictated by how a person is reared and has some relevance to one's spiritual life, but it is more specific about those things living around that person. A person who is moralistic may not be especially "religious," but may be very spiritual.

THE LESSON PLAN FORMAT

As you go out into the field to teach, you will find that your lesson plan is not just some magic hokum but something that is a guide you can't afford to be without. If you make a journey to some place you have not been before, you need guidelines or maps to follow. The lesson plan is your map for a successful journey to reach the desired destination.

There are as many possible ways to design lesson plans as there are teachers to teach them. One school of education has an adopted format that professional education professors teach as the "best" format to follow. That plan is easily followed, but perhaps the explication under each of the steps will be of benefit to you (see Figure 4.1).

Figure 4.1   Standard Lesson Plan Format

```
Class  _____
Date   _____

  I.   Objectives:

 II.   List of Materials and Supplies:

III.   Set Induction or Motivation:

IV.    Activities:
       Investigation:
       Discussion:
       Demonstration:
       Writing:
       Construction:

 V.    Provision for Individual Differences:

VI.    Closure and Follow-up:

VII.   Evaluation and Assessment:
```

I. Objectives

Write the following statement or something similar to begin your plan: "At the end of the lesson, students will [choose a verb from Bloom's verb list to signify the level at which your students will be working]" and then complete the statement. You will know that the objective is measurable if you state the proper verb from the Bloom list of objective verbs, but give the objective credibility by also locating it on one of Bloom's hierarchical categories and labeling it. Just remember here that the verb must be very specific from the list in Bloom's taxonomy, or you will get a general objective that cannot be measured, such as *understand*. Sometimes the more generic term seems to be easier to use, but if you are to assure that your students get the objective, a specific measurable verb will help you when you write some kind of assessment or evaluation to determine if the lesson was successful. It is virtually impossible to measure understanding until you view many times the person proving that understanding. It is very easy, on the other hand, to judge whether a student can apply a rule in a math problem or a chemistry experiment. So just remember to use the verbs in the Bloom list for each level of the domain in which you work.

II. List of Materials and Supplies

In this area of the plan, list all those items you will need to have on hand to accomplish the lesson objective. These are items that you have to take into the classroom with you and are not a regular part of the teaching tools generally available (e.g., chalk, eraser, chalkboard, overhead projectors). This listing seems rather simplistic and mundane, but if you have the items in a plan, it would be much more logical for you to have them available than if you had not thought of them prior to giving the lesson. If you come without the items, the students may think, "Aha, teacher is not prepared, so why should I worry about being prepared?" For instance, if you have no overhead projector and need to check one out at the audiovisual center, you should list it on your lesson plan to remind yourself that the machine has to go with you into the classroom. You should also make a list of the transparencies you will need to show on that projector. Again, this may seem commonsense and simplistic, but if you are teaching more than one subject a day, it is easy to forget to take care of these details if you are moving from one class to another. By compiling a list of materials needed for each class, you will be able to make the transitions smoothly and be ready to start class quickly. One of the basic principles discussed by Wong and Wong (1991) is that you have to start the class on time. If you have to go after something you have left behind, then the class can't start on time, and you have lost the battle of keeping the students' attention from the start of the class, when they are most receptive to what you have to say.

III. Set Induction or Motivation

List here exactly what you are going to do for today's motivation and for set induction for future lessons. For set induction, a teacher has to plan a few days ahead and use some tools such as bulletin boards, photos around the room, posters, banners, and so forth, to attempt to pique the students' interest without telling them what the next topic of study is going to be. It sets up a mood or a question that causes the students to wonder what is about to happen. You don't have to have a set induction for every lesson, but if such a thing will encourage the student to predict what might be coming, they will be more receptive to the ideas planned and later presented. For the day of the lesson, a teacher should bring in some kind of tangible artifact such as a framed historical document in a history class, or a tape of the *1812 Overture* if you are studying Napoleon, or pieces of fruit or any such tangible item to get better, more significantly thought-out discussions, writing, constructions, and so forth. As a general rule, verbal prompts are not nearly as thought-provoking as tangible ones for students. Your reading of the Martin Luther King, Jr., speech "I Have a Dream" to the class can be thought provoking, but the better way would be to show a video clip of King delivering the speech himself. That is the difference between a verbal and an artifactual stimulant.

IV. Activities

This is where you teach your lesson with well-planned activities that will enhance meeting your objective for the class on the day the plan is scheduled. You will have seatwork, lecture, homework, or whatever relates to the objective. Each activity should be set up for short intervals so that students will not become bored with the activities. "Less is more" is a very productive motto for a new teacher. Five 10-minute lessons, less time consuming and lower in depth, would be preferable to one 50-minute lesson, as long as you know what you want to do and say to make the quick 10-minute minilessons more enjoyable. Good lesson plans call for students to have five kinds of activities for each thematic-type unit to ensure that each student has five attempts to learn given objectives. We are not suggesting that you must do all five types of activity on a given day, but that, over a course of a few lessons on the same topic, you would have students do all the types of activities suggested. In this section, we describe these activities, which include *investigation, discussion, demonstration, writing,* and *construction.* We refer to this set of activities as IDDWC (Wyatt & Looper, 2003).

Investigation

The students gather data from whatever sources they can. This is the definitional stage of learning. This stage may include your lecture or your explanation, both of which are investigational for the student. It might include the students' searching for information in dictionaries, or in encyclopedias, or in magazine articles, or even in personal interviews or using the Internet. This is when they must begin to take the responsibility for their own background knowledge and for their own learning. This is when the students are first empowered with "real" knowledge. You can certainly list topics for groups to investigate. You can have then read the text orally. You can go over vocabulary words that are new to them. You can compare and contrast today's learning with something they have previously learned. This the time for you to help them learn to investigate. If you are a good facilitator, you will be able to place the students in good peer groups so they can teach each other. This is an excellent first step in assuring that no child will be left behind in getting the facts.

Discussion

After the students have done some investigation (including your lecture and question-and-answer sessions), they need to discuss their data among themselves to put what they have learned into a narrative format that they can understand. They will probably drop the "educationese" or teacher jargon and use the kind of jargon they and their peers understand. They need to discuss and perhaps repeat the lesson details to each other to reassure themselves that they know the material with which the topic deals. They will develop self-esteem by learning that they can talk about a topic they feel sure they understand because you have allowed them to empower themselves with their own investigational techniques. They have gathered data, and now they can prove it by showing that data to their peers. This is not a "teacher questions and student answers" discussion. If the teacher is involved at all, this becomes investigation. This must be student-to-student discussion.

You may prepare, and list on the lesson plan itself or on the chalkboard, some special questions that relate to the topic at hand, but over which you have not been exacting and specific in the investigative stage. Discussion that would resolve these kinds of questions allows students to engage in some critical-thinking skills and gives peer teaching (tutoring) in cooperative learning groups some special credence. This "talking time" or free discussion is very important to helping students focus on a topic and bring it home in such as way as to make them able to meet in any circles and be outstanding. Moving students from group to group to encourage their further participation will give them even more of that kind of assurance, but generally, the idea is to get them to trust their own peer group enough to be willing to participate in the discussions. A rubric could easily be designed to reference the amount of participation each member of a group contributes.

Demonstration

Once the students have investigated a topic and have discussed it in peer groups, they are ready to demonstrate their knowledge and its completeness. Working either with their peer groups in a cooperative demonstration or in an individual exercise, the students will design a program, chart, poster, or demonstration that they will give before the whole class, or another peer group within the class, to show that the demonstrators understand the topic at hand. Depending on what the topic is, they may go to the chalkboard to do a math problem, draw a cell, or diagram a sentence, or they may work with paints to mix a color, or they will demonstrate how to appropriately throw a football pass. They will be demonstrating their knowledge, and every member of the group should participate, showing in front of the class what they have gleaned from their discussion groups where they plan their demonstrations. The demonstration will confirm to them and to their teacher and peers that they know the topic. Remember that this demonstration should be done in an oral presentation so that each student within a discussion group gets a chance to speak before a group. This is another opportunity to show that no child is left behind.

Writing

Somewhere in the five-step IDDWC process, students must write on the topic at hand. You can have them do this by writing in a journal. They can write a composition, an essay answer on an examination, a letter to a friend concerning the topic, or a freewrite on the topic—whatever you can think of to give the students a chance to further voice knowledge of the topic. If you seem to bog down on the approach to writing, ask the students for input. You are certainly open by saying, "What kind of writing do you think we should do with this assignment to prove once more that you fully understand the topic being discussed and investigated?"

Construction

Students should construct something to show that they understand the topic. The writing assignment should not be considered the construction. The construction may be for the demonstration stage (a chart or a poster), but be sure that they also present the constructed item orally. Whatever they do, this is not a coloring project in which they color between your lines; they have to do the lines themselves. It is *their* construction project.

The activity section of your lesson, the IDDWC, if you choose to use the IDDWC plan, should be very carefully planned as student activity, using all of them somewhere in the series of lessons on a given topic. Your part in it as a teacher is really to help students with the investigative stage only. Asking questions and getting them to respond in class is not discussion. The students need to discuss among themselves. If you wish to do some evaluation after they have completed the activities, then initiate questions and answers from the group as a whole. The components of discussion, investigation, demonstration, writing, and construction are for the students to do so that they, and you, will know that they have mastered the topics covered by the objectives in your lessons or unit.

V. Provisions for Individual Differences

At this point in the lesson plan, the teacher needs to list activities for students with individual learning plans or special needs. If these students cannot do what the rest of the class is doing, what are you, the teacher, going to have them do to meet the same objective as the rest of the class? This we must do to fulfill the standards set by No Child Left Behind. If a student has special needs and doesn't have an individual learning plan for some reason, you still have the responsibility to see that the student, even if she can't speak English well, must participate if she is to learn the lesson. This is where you must learn to differentiate your lessons in such a way that the lessons reach each student.

VI. Closure and Follow-up

What are you going to do as a teacher to close today's lesson and to assure that the lesson is complete for the day? If you have a statement to close the assignment, place it on your lesson plan. Don't just yell at the students as they leave the room saying, "Be sure to. . . ." They won't get it. So close the lesson carefully. Then, after you have closed the topic for today, as a follow-up, you may want to give a take-home (homework) assignment that will give a little more instruction. It should be something to reinforce the day's lesson, using materials similar to those used in class. Its purpose is to give students further security in their knowledge. If you give homework, be sure to check it in some way to see that the students are learning and not mislearning information when they have done the work without your supervision.

VII. Evaluation and Assessment

The final stage of the lesson is to see what your students have done—to assess their progress and evaluate their learning. You can give a quiz. You can mark their written lesson. You can evaluate their demonstration. You can make a notation of their participation in the exercises you have outlined. You don't have to have written documentation for each day, but you should have an evaluation of some sort for every objective. In fact, it is a rule for some preservice teachers. For every objective they list, they must have at least one activity and one evaluation for that activity. One of the most precise and useful tools to complete this stage may be a rubric that you construct to list all the "points" that each student gets for completing each of the phases of the lesson.

Another benefit of using the IDDWC format is that you can easily go back over your plans and identify how you have met individual needs. Table 4.1 shows how each part of the design addresses many of the multiple intelligences identified by Gardner.

Table 4.1   Activities Planning Matrix

	Investigation	Discussion	Demonstration	Writing	Construction
Verbal/ Linguistic	X	X	X	X	X
Logical/ Mathematical		X		X	
Musical/ Rhythmic		X			
Visual/ Spatial			X	X	X
Bodily/ Kinesthetic					X
Interpersonal		X			X
Intrapersonal	X				
Naturalistic					
Spiritual/ Existential			X	X	
Moral			X	X	

FINDING YOUR OWN FORMAT

Using the lesson plan format we have just described will help you see how what you are doing meets the needs of your diverse students. It may not be practical for you to use every day for every class, but you do need to use it often as a means of checking your ability to plan thoroughly and effectively. As you mature as a teacher, you may be more comfortable using a format like Figure 4.2.

Figure 4.2   Personlized Lesson Plan Format

Class:	Unit:	Date:
Objective	Procedures	Materials
Evaluation		
Introduction		
Lesson		
Closing		

The thing you will discover after a few years of teaching is that the format you are most comfortable with is the one you choose to meet your needs most effectively. How much structure do you need? What does your principal require? How can you keep track of the objectives you have covered? What kinds of reminders do you need to make your classroom operate efficiently? Remember that an effective teacher has a plan. He knows what he wants his students to learn. He knows how he is going to try to help them learn that material. He also knows that, if he has planned instruction that meets many levels of student needs and addresses the standards required by the state and local district, he will be successful. Students will learn, and each class will have a sense of direction and purpose. Bob, a very demanding yet well-planned English teacher, said, "I knew that I had done a good job when at the end of class, one student would turn to another and say, 'This class is always so short!'" That is the best reward for time spent on designing lesson plans.

JOURNAL TOPICS

- Take your plan book and plot in one semester or one grading period. Be sure to include all holidays, special events, and shortened school days. Plot places that would be good for having students take a major test or complete a major assignment.
- Think of a unit of study you might plan for your subject area. Prioritize the skills or materials your students need to learn. Identify the most critical items or concepts, things that it would be nice for your students to know. Finally, identify things that you enjoy but that your students might not find interesting or relevant.
- Brainstorm benefits of using a detailed plan like the IDDWC.
- Brainstorm lessons that might need less detail.
- Practice designing lesson plans using both formats discussed in this chapter.

CHAPTER FIVE

Making Assessment Work

A licia Jacobs got an appointment with the high school principal to discuss Alicia's student scores. Alicia was frantic because she was a novice teacher and there was so much emphasis on the students passing the exit exams for her class. Her students were not doing well at all.

"What can I do to get my students to be more serious when they take the tests that we are required to give? I have been teaching right to the state's list of required materials for my class. I have given them every benefit of my good preparation in the subject matter, but I have also been giving them some tests that I have made up on the topics in the standards. I have made the tests both multiple choice and constructed-response essay answers. My students just don't do well on the tests," Alicia said.

The principal had several relevant questions. She asked, "First, Alicia, are you sure you are teaching at a level where each of the students in your class can understand the material? Do you plan your lessons in such a way that you and your students know at what level they are working? Bloom's Taxonomy can help you to know that for certain by the verb that you use as you write each objective. For instance, if you are using the verb *understand*, there is really no way that you can measure understanding because it occurs at so many levels. Do you do any diagnostic testing before you start a series of lessons? If not, how do you know how to plan your lessons? If all of the students know the material you are teaching, they will be bored if you spend more than just a cursory look at the material as a matter of review.

"Have you done any differentiation planning for those in your classes who may be performing at a substandard level or a higher level than for the grade level you are teaching? Begin thinking of having more than one objective on the same topic with differentiated approaches to accomplishing those objectives at the various levels. Remember, though, that if the students are substandard, you don't just assign fewer problems or fewer questions, you make their lesson different so it will fit their needs. Or just because you have a bright, gifted student, don't pile on extra assignments of the same kind that you are giving the other students. Plan special, differentiated assignments for those students.

"You know, Alicia, we are now into a period of very high stakes testing in our profession. We are called upon to get our students ready to take exit exams that will show that we have met the requirements of No Child Left Behind legislation, the state standards, our own school's standards, and our own standards as well-prepared educators. I haven't answers for you as to how you must do this learning and testing, but I hope the questions I asked can stimulate you to look carefully at what you are doing in your class. If you need to stop and change your processes, that is a good thing to do. I want you to excel as the wonderful teacher that I knew you would be when I hired you. Just try to make yourself more aware of the students' needs and their levels, then you will fulfill your obligations much more easily," Mrs. Adams said. "I know this may be overwhelming, but look at the big picture and then take small steps each day to work toward helping your students grow. It isn't going to happen overnight, but as long as I know you are working toward that, I will be pleased with your performance as a teacher."

Assessment is one of the most difficult things a teacher does. The teacher has to assign materials so that she can grade (i.e., assess or evaluate) her students in order to know what they are doing toward meeting desired objectives. That kind of assessment is valuable for determining how students are doing, but it also tells the teacher how she is doing as a teacher. There is a great difference between teaching subject matter and teaching students, and therein lies the answer about how much a teacher must be involved in assessing her students. Alicia Jacobs in the above scenario needs to keep this idea foremost in her mind as she continues to prepare her students for their required evaluations toward the end of the school year.

STANDARDIZATION IN ASSESSMENT

For several decades, the only "good" kind of testing, as far as many legislators and media reporters have been concerned, has been standardized testing. Advisors in the school enrollment process often use those standardized assessments for placement, suggesting that this is the best method for self-investigation, for comparative purposes of publicizing their schools, and for determining how one school stacks up against others. There is nothing wrong with that approach if the intent for such testing is honorable. However, often students are judged *solely* on standardized, norm-referenced tests (even those made for you to use as daily or weekly tests that come with your teachers' guide to your textbook) rather than criterion-referenced tests in which you, the teacher, test students on what you have taught rather than what textbook authors feel should be taught from their texts or what large testing companies feel should be known by people the age of your students. Granted, their material is well-researched, but it should not be held as sacrosanct just because it is well-researched and available. Good assessment looks at many evaluative pieces, including both norm-referenced and criterion-referenced tests. Such an evaluative process reminds one of a patient going to a physician. The doctor pokes and feels and listens to symptoms before he makes a decision on how to treat his patient. Often, he decides that his immediate tests cannot answer his questions so he sends his patient for lab work, for x-rays, and other kinds of data-gathering devices. He even has to look at the patient's environmental surroundings to determine what effect the environment might have on his patient. Such questions as to what a patient eats, how the patient has been sleeping, and other environmental factors can certainly affect his treatment plans. After the physician has gathered all this data with his criterion-referenced techniques, he uses the norm-referenced-type data so that he can be accurate in his diagnosis and treatment of what ails his patient.

The materials that you are supplied with along with your text may be good materials. Such preprepared materials are not the only materials that you should use. Novice teachers are often overloaded on work, being involved as they are with teaching new-content discipline materials, learning names of students and judging capabilities of various students, and trying to differentiate the process for the different students in her class. They are constantly aware that they need to try to please a mentor teacher and a principal, both of whom have their own ideas on how to run a classroom and teach the students. Not only must novice teachers adjust to teaching, they must go home from the classroom to such nonteaching duties as maintaining regular household chores, pleasing a spouse, and perhaps taking care of children, all while trying to make a teacher's salary meet the cost of living. Sometimes teachers will turn to these prepackaged tests just to give themselves a breather. As long as you realize that standardized, norm-referenced tests are just indicators of how your students are getting along with what has been normed as good for their age or for the text involved, you will be fine. But you just *have* to know that there are other methods and other angles you can pursue, even as a new teacher, to make what you are assessing and evaluating more authentically acceptable to you and to your students.

USING FORMATIVE ASSESSMENTS

The *formative* assessment is very valuable, but it is often left out of the evaluation lineup. This is a diagnostic test that shows the teacher where the student stands on the knowledge of the subject matter the teacher has to teach. It is not designed to be graded. It gives information to the teacher and does not put the student in any kind of jeopardy because of its design. Students will argue that a test is a test, and should be counted for them as a grade in the grade book. They argue that if they are going to take the time to take the test, the grade they made, whether high or low, should count. Those who do very well on the test will be more adamant about its being counted as a score. For the teacher to gain the needed information that formative assessment can provide, he will have to explain the purpose of the assessment so that students will understand they need to do their best, yet not expect a grade. This may be a challenge for a teacher operating in a test-driven environment.

A teacher must make absolutely clear to the student how test-driven our society is and what exactly is riding on the test that will be administered. The student needs to know what a test of any kind is to accomplish. If it is diagnostic, tell the students that you just need to know where he is located in the content you are about to cover. If an end-of-the-year standardized exit exam, he should be aware that failing the test could cause him to have to repeat a class. Students need to know where they stand. Every possible form of assessment has to be valuable to the student as well as the teacher.

Formative tests tell the student what should come from the lessons the teacher teaches, just as an objective written on the chalkboard at the front of the room should let the student know what will be done in the classroom each day. Every test or assessment, even if it is a standardized test, should be formative (give some information) in some way.

Bloom and colleagues (Bloom, Englehart, Furst, Hill, & Krathwohl, 1956) note that a teacher cannot take a student from a level at which he is capable and move him two steps higher to an area to which he has not progressed naturally through instruction. The student has to go through the steps one at a time (see Chapter 4 for a discussion of Bloom in more detail). Education students often ask in pedagogy classes, "How do we determine the level of a student's ability?" A formative test is the answer to that question. It keeps a novice teacher, or even an experienced teacher who has forgotten, from rambling around a topic when the students are not ready to move to that topic. It also keeps a teacher from boring students by rehashing a topic they already know. Assessment of each objective's desired results makes an awareness of how each student is progressing. Students can do work that fools the teacher about how much they know. There is always the chance that Mom read the book and wrote the report. Perhaps Dad or a girlfriend has helped Johnny with his math homework. The teacher feels rather smug about how Johnny has moved along so well. Administering a test will reveal the real Johnny's ability to do the problems or read a book.

What is the benefit of using formative tests? Students working below their capability level may behave in a disruptive manner because they are expected to do materials too far below their comprehension levels. They see this work as useless, maybe even as "busy" work. Or, on the other hand, if the work is too far above their capability, the students are bored and disruptive. They think that they can't perform at the level expected, and they just decide they may as well misbehave. So what is the answer for both the novice and the long-term teacher? A diagnostic test! It gives the teacher something that sets the level at which the test taker can work. Once you have analyzed the student, diagnosed her level of capability on a given topic, you can write objectives that help that student accomplish reachable goals (Mager, 1984; Moore, 1999). You don't always have to use a test format. You might want to have students write to a prompt that asks them to write about information they need to know. You might want to design a crossword puzzle or a set of problems to be worked as you check roll. There are many ways to give diagnostic tests without labeling them as tests. Every activity that the students do can produce information that shows whether they have gotten the content. At that point the teacher can choose to re-teach or move on to a new topic.

Secondary and middle school students are accustomed to the testing process, and they will expect a grade for every attempt they make to do any exercise, even diagnostic ones. Students often ask, and you *will* have the question asked of you, "Why do we have to do this if we aren't going to get a grade?" They have become accustomed to a reward system for all that they do, and if that is not present, they just don't want to do the work. You will find that students may, in fact, just slough off the diagnostic because it doesn't offer them the reward of a grade. It is too bad that they don't realize that all you as the teacher are trying to do is make their learning better by prescribing material that fills in any deficiencies they may have. If they slough off the diagnosis, then you may be misprescribing. When students are asked to do materials in which they are already competent, they will cry, "Boredom!" and bedlam could result, or at the very least you could get unabashed apathy. Both are difficult for any teacher to contend with, but especially the new teacher. Because you need the information in order to plan meaningful teaching and learning activities, you may find that giving the students some kind of rubric with point scores on it as a completion grade for these types of testing make the diagnostics a little more acceptable.

USING SUMMATIVE EVALUATIONS

Another kind of evaluation is the one that usually follows an assigned set of materials designed for the student to master. That form of assessment is a *summative* assessment. That assessment is designed for the teacher to give some kind of award for its accomplishment, usually an award in the form of a grade. As you examine your objectives and your lesson plans, follow the concepts you learned in your testing and measurement classes. Make sure that you teach what you test and only test what you teach. Even though (more often than we would like to admit) teachers often create their evaluation procedures as they near the end of a unit of study, they will be more successful in matching their evaluations to actual instruction and learning activities if they think about what they need to evaluate early in the unit rather than later. Testing is more authentic if you plan your evaluation and the criteria on which you will judge it early in the designing and implementation of your unit of study.

OVERCOMING APATHY: MAKING LESSONS AUTHENTIC AND USING ALTERNATIVE ASSESSMENT

With good diagnosis and written objectives to guide instruction that meet the needs for each learner (who can often be grouped with others who have the same diagnosis), the teacher can determine where the student stands and at least offer differentiated lessons on the basis of individual student needs. This is a tough assignment, and even master teachers balk at having to design such individual lessons, if they have been trained in the modernist perspective, which claims that teachers are "ones who impart knowledge." Teachers trained in this type of pedagogy feel as if they should try to pry open their students' heads and pour in the knowledge they need. The newer postmodern (and even the constructivist approach, in which students build on their scaffold of learning) would be to have the teacher act as a facilitator who plans instruction, who produces an effective learning environment, and who allows the students to learn on their own through the use of cooperative learning or individualized, differentiated (Tomlinson, 2001) learning activities.

Establishing authentic lessons that students care about, and then using good testing or good alternative methods of assessment, helps abate student apathy, if not eradicate it. It is not unusual for there to be as many as 10 groups going in a classroom of 20 students. Each group would be doing something different, based on the IDDWC activity materials discussed in Chapter 4. Those who know little about the subject, according to the diagnostic testing, are at the "I" stage, investigating the topic in their texts, on the Internet, in an encyclopedia, or from trade books recommended by the teacher. Some of them, according to the discipline being taught, may be out interviewing if they are, for instance, studying World War II in their history course. If you really want students to know the subject so that it is authentic, teaching them to use interviews for the *I-Search* techniques of Ken Macrorie (1980) will be much more valuable than all the extraneous reading a student will do. If the student who investigates finally gets to the Vietnam conflict in American history, she will then feel competent to apply knowledge gained firsthand about World War II to Vietnam, and to confirm the application, she may be interested in interviewing Vietnam veterans. She may learn that the kinds of battles and fighting that she found for World War II were totally different from the experiences learned from the Vietnam veterans she interviews. The point is, by providing authentic learning experiences, I-Searches, you are allowing students to learn and apply what they are learning. This type of application is the kind of assessment that is called *alternative* assessment. The students who investigated could then write some kind of reflection on learning using the "W" (writing) of the IDDWC. The reflection may certainly be some further drop into diagnosis, but it could also easily be seen as a possibility for summative evaluation, because the student who learns authentically and applies skills used in authentic learning to her life has taken an important step to true learning—lifelong learning.

Authentic learning opens the doorway for continued learning. For example, those students who have authentically learned about World War II and Vietnam will have a better understanding of modern warfare and could be encouraged to apply what they have learned to the recent example of Desert Storm or Iraq. Of course, more intense and authentic learning will occur if they interview family or community members who have been involved in previous wars as well as in the latest war. They will learn how technology has changed this event. For instance, whereas World

War II took 5 years to end the conflict, Desert Storm took only a few days.

Those students have now learned true application as part of the process of learning. It is also likely that if students have gone through the Investigation and the Writing stages of the IDDWC, there should be no problem in their doing the *Discussion* stage, in which they get to meet in cooperative learning groups to discuss what they have learned and try to tie it to what their peers know. They solidify their knowledge to the point that their cooperative group may be able to *Demonstrate* their group knowledge on the topic of modern warfare by presenting what they have learned to the entire class. They may need to make a poster of their findings (the *Construction* stage) to make their knowledge more appealing and authentic to their peers, who can also make a visual connection to the information they have also gathered. Each of the activities is alternative assessment once the Investigative stage has ended. You, as the teacher, might even be involved in that Investigative stage by doing some lecturing, clarifying some points that the students question, and working with them in their cooperative learning groups. You will always have a place to cooperate with them, even as "just" a facilitator.

It is important to note at this juncture on the lesson planning, that just because the students are in the DDWC stages after you have already passed by Investigation, the teacher may need to jump into the learning at any time if the class is going astray or if the information seems to be faulty according to the textual material they are reading for their investigation. However, if you do step back into the process and it is a planned foray into the process, then you have to return to the Investigation stage again. The teacher can only be a part of investigation. If student-teacher discussion occurs with the teacher leading the discussion, then that is not the Discussion stage, but you have reverted to the Investigation stage. Discussion must be among peer groups. Remember the IDDWC items are not hierarchical.

USING PORTFOLIOS AS AN ALTERNATIVE ASSESSMENT

Portfolios are another way for your students to "Demonstrate" what they know and share that knowledge with you, the teacher, and with peers, parents, and other interested parties. Portfolios are alternative assessments, and as such, give you another avenue of "testing" and "grading" the students. If you prepare a check sheet for what should be in the portfolio or do a rubric that can give you a set of scores, you have something numerical to record in your grade book, even though the product is an alternative assessment.

Portfolios are also interesting for you to read. They may become individualistic in their reflective statements, as long as you don't require the students to do rigidly formatted reflections. If you allow them to respond truly to what they have gathered and want to show you in their portfolios, then the portfolio is a wonderful assessment tool.

USING DIRECT ASSESSMENT

As the postmodern era approaches, those tasks that may be evaluated for their meaningfulness or their ability to be integrated within the curriculum, offer chances for alternative assessments. That kind of assessment will have greater meaning for the student (Briggs, Tully, & Stiefer, 1998). These assessments are often nothing more than observations that you, as the teacher, may take note of in your grade book so that you can see that the students have accomplished the goals and objectives you hoped they would, either as individuals or in cooperative groups, or perhaps even as a whole class. That kind of assessment is valuable because you know from it, at least, that the students have engaged in learning that meets their individual needs. This type of assessment is used extensively in elementary classrooms, but it is harder to use in secondary classes because you have less time and more students. However, you can devise a schedule to follow in using observation. For example, if your students are forming cooperative learning groups, you might closely observe and note the actions of members in one or two groups per class. This provides rich information, and, with a little practice, you will be able to gather it confidently.

Researchers are finding that students are more accurately evaluated if the evaluations are conducted in authentic rather than contrived environments (Briggs et al., 1998). Having a student understand the material being taught or studied is far more valuable for the student than scoring high on a standardized test. As we get more into individualized lessons for all students, similar to the individual learning plans written for special students, any interaction with real life is preferable to those situations that offer nothing with which the students can identify. Critical thinking is more likely to occur with application in an authentic context. Knowing how to use a process of learning is a better indication of learning than highly rated standardized scores. Those students who can perform well on standardized tests are often able to adapt to any learning style or learning situation, perhaps even more easily than those who cannot or do not score high on standardized tests because of the critical thinking skills that are required on most standardized tests. Those students who do well are at the high application or the analysis level in Bloom's cognitive domain. Noncriterion tests are generally more closely connected to the classroom teacher who has taught the material, and having taught it and observed the students through that teaching, she makes the test appropriate for specific material. This generally does not require nearly so much critical thinking, but rather the regurgitation of material presented in the class. When the teacher is able to observe the goals of her learning objectives being realized in a real-world environment, the result of such learning is much more credible for the student and the teacher. We hope that, at some point in our history, legislators and media moguls will realize the truth of this important concept.

USING A RUBRIC

In education circles the word *rubric* has become very important. Most of you who have completed pedagogy classes understand a rubric, but for those who may have forgotten or who have attained your certification alternatively, some material may be worthy of your consideration. Exactly what is a rubric, and when do you use one? The rubric is a more objective way of looking at a subjective kind of assessment, particularly when one is judging written papers (reports, journals, reflections, etc.) or essay-type examination questions. The teacher makes a list of those items that she will look for, specifically, within the written document. The rubric will detail what items must be addressed for a student to receive an A, what fewer items a teacher will accept for the student to earn a B, and so forth (see Figure 5.1). The rubric must be presented to the students before the paper or the essays are evaluated so that the teacher doesn't just make spur-of-the-moment or biased decisions on what is good, or what is not quite so good, or what is just passable. You create your rubric before giving the assignment; then no matter who the student is or how differentiated that student's work may be, there is less bias in recording the grade. Make the rubric simple and to the point, but be sure that both you and the student using the rubric understand exactly what is required. Will you accept mere mention of the words, or must you have a certain number of details? Must a subject be highly or briefly detailed in the written answer? If students know what is expected of them and if you have talked about the kinds of things that you look for in your rubric, students can meet those expectations. Of course, they think that the true/false, matching, fill-in-the-blank, or multiple-choice tests are easier, but if you want to test their knowledge and understand how their thinking (metacognitive) process works, essays with rubrics for scoring are an excellent way to evaluate student learning.

USING PEER JUDGMENTS

Sometimes you may ask the peers in the room to make judgments of performance by the students. You have to be aware that there may be some bias on the part of the peer evaluators. They are still youngsters with few life experiences, so their judgments may not be as complete as they need to be. However, you may find that students accept the critiques of their peers with some, perhaps higher, level of appreciation because they know that their peers have gone through the same kinds of evaluations or assessments. When your students are engaged with the IDDWC activity sections of your lesson plans, they may all be working at different levels on different planes. Most often you can have small peer groups engaged in cooperative learning situations. That is fair because they can see the trees without looking through your forest of experiences. They are much more tolerant of some kinds of errors made by their peers than you might be, but they often are harder on the presenters in class than you, the teacher, would be. They have been in the same position, so they are not as tolerant of

Figure 5.1   This rubric shows items the teacher feels necessary for a good presentation. She checks off the preferred items as the student presents them. If a student has all the items checked, he earns a high score, with his score declining for each item left unattended.

Poetry Lesson Rubric

— The student participated in interpretation and correcly constructed a cinquain, using the nature foundation and the exact formula in syllabic count.

— The student participated some in discussion and constructed a cinquain-like poem, but varied the poem from the exact formula.

— The student did not participate in the discussion but wrote something to turn is as a poem.

— The student neither participated in the discussion nor turned in a written poetry example.

Assessment Rubric on Writing

— The student wrote the narrative in such a way that showed understanding of the concept of the mathematical formula and solved the word problem correctly using the concept.

— The student wrote a narrative but did not demonstrate that he knew the concept. Did write the correct answer, but did not use the process we discussed in class.

— The student solved the problem using a route different from our plan discussed in class.

— The student neither wrote the narrative nor solved the problem correctly, though he made an effort for solution.

— There was no participation from the student on the writing or on the process or on attempting to solve the problem.

---

goofing off or sugarcoating or laughing through a presentation that is supposed to reflect the knowledge of those in the class. Students are excellent critics, for the most part, and the one being evaluated may take the evaluation more seriously if a peer makes that evaluation.

When you ask students to evaluate their peers' work, the evaluators should take the responsibility of making written reflections that justify their evaluations and of offering suggestions to the presenters. This ensures that they use critical thinking for their evaluations. They should never be allowed to do what teachers often do, just put an A, B, C, D, or F on a paper. The process of peer evaluation makes students much more aware of what you do when you evaluate each of them. Also understand that you will need to train your students and model for them the behavior that good peer evaluators exhibit. This would be a good time to teach and demonstrate the qualities of tact and discretion.

SO WHAT ABOUT ASSESSMENT?

However you get into assessing a student, you know that the way a student performs on an assignment or a standardized test is a reflection on you. That is a fact that you can't change; you are the teacher. However, you have in your knowledge base the pedagogical skills to make judgments about your students and their scores (grades). Alternative methods of assessment may answer some of the needs. If your school does have a policy that requires that every assignment have a numerical rating, you can set up your rubrics so that fully meeting certain expectations equals a certain numerical value. In that way, you are able to establish a numerical rating for the school and for your grade reporting. With a rubric on file for each assignment, you are able to justify your scores to those who have a need to know (i.e., parents or school administrators) how you came up with specific grade scores for your students.

Assessment and evaluation are not easy tasks. Teachers seem to have to justify their students' scores. It is much easier and much fairer for the teacher and the students if the teacher decides in advance what she wants from the students, tells them what she expects, then scores their papers and tests accordingly. Sometimes a mentor teacher is a good source for helping you decide what you would like to do in your classroom, but ultimately, the decision rests with you. As you work toward effective assessment, remember that developing this skill is a process. The second year you will do better, create more rubrics, and understand assessment more fully. Each year you will gain confidence as you practice your skills. Try not to let state-mandated testing and the need for authentic assessment become burdens. Allow yourself time, just as you would your students, to master the art of assessment.

JOURNAL TOPICS

- Discuss the method of assessment that is most appealing to you, telling why it seems appropriate for your classes.
- Describe other areas of alternative assessment that you could use in your classes.
- Make a rubric that will help you assess your next class assignment; then use that rubric as part or all of a student's score on that project.
- Brainstorm a list of other methods of assessment.

CHAPTER SIX

Making Technology Work for Enhanced Learning

Technology is a tool that can be your friend or your foe in the classroom. It can enhance the knowledge base of your students. It can give them Internet connections all around the world. It can be a headache for you when it comes to control of the system. However, if you accept the challenge of learning and using technology, it can become one of the most valuable tools for critical thinking and good learning.

One unfortunate problem of using technology is that many schools and many students do not have adequate finances to set up a good technological system. If you happen to be in a school where most students have computers at their fingertips, then you will be very lucky. Should you be in a school in lower-income community, you will not be able to have homework assigned using the Internet or computer searches. Teachers will just have to use the tools at their disposal. Many homes will have a computer available but will have numerous family members fighting over the use of the system, so when you make assignments, even if you know your student has a home computer and Internet capability, you will need to realize that any assignments you make will have to have some advanced planning to give students time to have access to the home computer.

For those of you who wind up in a school where the economic base is higher, you may find the computer and Internet as ready tools for homework assignments. In some districts, teachers are required to have a Web page and a parent portal on which notices of homework, grades, and other essential parent information may be posted. If that is the case, you can do all kinds of wonderful things, such as scanning student work for display on the parent portal page so the parents can see individual assignments that their child has contributed to the class. Such programs take a great deal of teacher time but may be worth the effort. There can be general material that, with one-time input, can be sent to all parents, but there may be days when you have to do special writing to several individual parents. If this kind of approach and program is available, you should be certain that you can keep the Web page up to date and working before you begin the program. Parents may not be everyday participants, but if they want to check on things in your classroom, the Web page should always be up to date. Secondary and middle school students will not be too concerned about their work being shown to their parents and in fact may not want it shown. Sometimes, however, especially when the work is not as well done as it should be or when you have behavioral issues with which you might need parental support, such reporting on a daily basis is good leverage for the teacher. Realize, however, that anything that is put into a computer should be handled well, because any angry or out-of-focus material that is printable from a home computer may be something that can be used against you should some problem arise.

We have found that the best use of the Internet as a tool is when the teacher is the facilitator, the one who sets up the cues for good learning. It is a wonderful tool for the authentic lesson when students are allowed to investigate (see Chapter 4 for the IDDWC) for themselves and learn those pieces of knowledge that they feel they need to know. Of course, students need to be inspired by the teacher to want to find authentic material; but once the teacher has made an assignment, the student can feel very much at home searching the Internet to find every possible clue on the topic assigned. Having generally grown up with the Internet, most students by middle school are more adept than many of their teachers at finding information on the Internet. If your students are from an affluent community and you need some information and cannot find it or even cannot take time to find it, just mention it to your students, and you will be astounded at the data that they can find and send to you in forwarded e-mail or by printing it for you. Sometimes this kind of effort is a good teaching tool in itself. Once, Alex needed some background for a student to prepare for an academic team competition, and he could find nothing of relevance. He told his class, and at a computer time for the students, within minutes, Alex had enough data to give the academic team member some material that would help with the problem.

STUDENTS BECOME ACTIVELY INVOLVED

The more a person is involved with her own learning, the more she is likely to learn. It is good for a student to explore all the avenues she can think of when she is trying to find knowledge on a given subject. For instance, a student who studies about the great number of immigrants who came to America and had to enter through Ellis Island may look to the Internet address www.ellisislandrecords.org for material. There may be a way she could make a connection in searching for one of her own ancestors, or at least those with the same surname, who might have been one of those coming through the Ellis Island list. What a good, authentic way to learn about the history of immigration. The added bonus may well hit very close to the student's heart if she finds possible real family connections among those listed making their way to America, although the immigrants who came that route may not be listed under their correct names because many of them had their hard-to-spell foreign names changed by the Ellis Island workers, who could only guess at the spellings. Likely, the name they picked up on the Island will be the same as the current one the family uses, however, so there may still be that connection and that learning. Such an interactive search could prove much more relevant to that student than her looking up information in an encyclopedia. She could never find the Ellis Island lists in an encyclopedia. Technology brings its own headaches to the classroom, but it also brings the potential of great rewards for both student and teacher.

Most schools today will have access to computers somewhere in the school even if they don't have classroom computers with an Internet hookup. As a novice teacher, you would do well to see the school librarian early in your new assignment and find out where your students may get access to computers, how you would go about scheduling such an event, and how often you may expect to have such access.

STUDENTS MAY ASK QUESTIONS

Suppose the material that you are teaching in your secondary language arts class requires students to understand a preposition. Many students may be able to name the prepositions using the elementary way of finding them. Some may think of the box with the plank lying next to it, and anything that the plank can do to the box shows that you have found the prepositions, such as *in* the box, *by* the box, *from* the box, *near* the box, and so forth. However, it is much easier just to feed the word *preposition* to the search mechanism of the Internet driver. You will find the list and the explanations all made out for you. That is one of the strongest arguments against having students memorize such a list: information like this is so available that your students' memory work could be so much better served by remembering items that are not readily available via the Internet. This was a very simplistic example, but it gives an idea of the usefulness of the computer and the Internet in the classroom if you have such capabilities. Even if there is just one computer, and it is at the teacher's desk, you could allow your students to use that computer unless the school has a policy against the student using the teacher's computer. If your school has such a policy, you could work around it, for instance, by finding a site that discusses prepositions and, if you have a projector to which you can hook your computer, projecting it on a screen for all the students to see. Many schools have such projectors available. If one is not available, perhaps you could write a grant to get one for your own classroom. Many are priced at less than $1,000. Speak with your school's grant person if one is on campus or to your principal if a grant writer is not on campus to ask for help in writing a grant to get your classroom a projector that will connect to your computer.

GLOBAL CONNECTIONS

An e-mail connection on the Internet literally opens up worlds of opportunities for learning. If your students are studying world history or current events, think of the kind of learning they could have by contacting someone in the area that you are studying in class. Mark, a high school geography teacher, has his students contact a person in a country they have each drawn from a hat. He has them connect with their selected country's secretary of state office, their United Nations representative, and the mayor's offices in at least three cities in the country to get some authentic, firsthand knowledge of the country they are investigating. The connections have been generally well-received, with only one or two exceptions, and when the students told their contacts what they were doing and why, most of the people with whom they corresponded sent letters and even gifts so that they would know the investigated country better. One student received a set of travel guidebooks from the country's director of tourism. One received some pieces of that country's currency to display before the class in a demonstration that was a part of the IDDWC assignment. One received a complete wardrobe that would be worn in that country. He received a shirt and pants made of silk, a turban, a pair of ceremonial shoes, and some jewelry that a young man would wear to a coming-of-age celebration in that country. Several received formal letters signed by the heads of state. Mark's point was to try to determine if the world was truly just one global community in which people wanted to communicate with others. The response to that question from him and his students was positive. The Internet was used for much of the communication, but formal letters also became necessary on many occasions. Thank-you notes for the gifts had to be written in a formal way, so students had the opportunity to do more than just connect with the global community through the cyber connections. Such organizations or persons would be overwhelmed if many students contacted them in this way, but you could brainstorm with your students and see if they can come up with an idea to make a global connection. You will be surprised at how well-versed many are and how creative their ideas for contact can be.

Always use care about any connections that are on the Internet. There are many unscrupulous people who respond to connections. Involve yourself in viewing what your students might be viewing on the screen. This is certainly a place for the teacher to be involved in the investigation stage (see Chapter 4).

COOPERATIVE EFFORTS
IN THE CLASSROOM

Most classrooms are not overly equipped with computers and connections, even though most schools recognize their value and are moving rapidly toward that goal. In the facilitator role, the teacher has many opportunities to set up cooperative learning groups to work together and use the Internet and the computer on given days each week. Students set their group goals on the basis of the teacher's stated objectives for the unit, and then they take some time to plan how to use their class period most effectively during the computer time. They also have to set down rules and time slots for the various roles for the use of the computer. One advantage to having cooperative groups is that all the people in that group learn the knowledge that the group gains while each learns to use the computer effectively.

Some kind of journal writing should be connected with computer usage as an exercise in problem solving. Each student sees a problem from a different perspective or from diverse backgrounds. If they each write what they have found and reflect upon that finding, you as the teacher can assess what they are learning by reading their journals. One of the most gratifying learning accomplishments that students have when they use computers and the Internet is that they have to plan and use good strategies. If the first search or first search driver does not give them what they need, they have to go to Plan B for another effort. That moving from Plan A to Plan B is part of the strategies of learning. The computer with Internet allows them to learn to use the search strategies freely.

THE COMPUTER AS A TEACHING TOOL

Conventional teaching has so much tradition accompanying it that many teachers don't want to get away from it because it is a safety net. The computer is a tool, just as a pencil, some chalk, and a ballpoint pen are tools. The computer will not replace the teacher, even if the class is an online operation. Someone has to guide the material on such a plan, and teachers will be the ones doing that. One factor in using the computer well is that you know you are preparing your students to function well in today's fast-moving, mobile world. If you teach students how to use the computer, how to search databases, what computer etiquette to use, then you will have prepared your students for the lifelong learning that has become such a strong demand on teachers of this new century.

Another benefit of using technology is the wide array of subjects students can explore and learn. There are interactive televisions stations available so that students may take courses not offered at their own schools. This gives the student in Small School, USA, the same benefit that those who attend metropolitan schools have. There is also special computer software available for virtually any course you teach. Many textbook publishers furnish a teacher copy of a CD-ROM that has information, art, and other details to enhance presentation of the materials in the text. Some learners now study conversational Spanish using computer software and a textbook. They work on the course when it is convenient for them to do so, and they learn at a pace that is comfortable for them. Many colleges offer computer-generated and online courses as accredited material for undergraduate and graduate degrees, homebound students, or for students who have to study by an alternative approach to learning. Several universities advertise that a student can complete full degrees up through a doctorate at their institutions without ever or at least rarely having to attend even a lecture day on campus. A computer is patient and can give the lesson to a student at that student's pace. It can offer the student feedback. It can give practical instruction with minimal interference from teachers. It can also allow the student to delve more deeply into a topic he may find interesting and want to pursue long after the scheduled classroom lesson is completed. Such programs may be costly if they are appropriately designed by the person doing the teaching, as they are very time consuming to create.

HOW DOES A NEW
TEACHER GET INVOLVED?

One of the first things a new teacher should do upon entering into a contract with a school is to meet with the best teachers and ask what they are doing technologically in their classrooms. Then the teacher can take what they are doing and either adapt it for her own students' needs or decide to do something differently to meet the needs of the course she teaches. A teacher can build an entire curriculum on the basis of computerized course work, or she can set up a blended course with a minimal amount of computer work until she is accustomed to the school and the youngsters. Before adopting such teaching technology, it is best to determine how savvy your students are with computers and how many of them have a computer available in their homes. Gain as much information as you can about computers and their operations before you enter into your school year.

Your job may be so much easier as a lecturer if one of your computers is connected to a large monitor so that all the youngsters can see your material at one time as you speak. These projectors are usually available in schools and can be reserved from your computer lab or media center for classroom use if you don't have your own in your classroom. Occasionally, some schools with additional money to spend place such units in each classroom so that students and teachers have more access to that form of technology. From this technology both teachers and students can use PowerPoint to present a multitude of presentations using photos, music, and various color and prints on computer slides to make the lessons more interesting to learn. Learning takes place more easily and quickly. A picture and a word together bring quicker learning results that last a great deal longer. If students can construct a PowerPoint presentation, use the construction stage of the lesson plan to build such a presentation (see Chapter 4). This will be good for building self-esteem and enhancing learning with that student empowerment.

One Web location that seems very appropriate for use in your classroom is www.educationworld.com/a_tech/. You can find hundreds of tools that will set your students to thinking and studying. Such great motivation is rarely seen in classrooms. In looking under "Edgar Allan Poe," Rachel, a secondary English teacher, found that there were several video clips. One was on Poe himself. One was of his writing of "The Raven." One was about Baltimore when Poe lived there. She looked into their history category and found hundreds of free items that could be used just by clicking on them and either projecting them for your class or printing segments that would be useful. If nothing else, just viewing this material for yourself will inspire you to enjoy teaching the material you find. It is certainly teacher-motivational. Another Web address that discusses the use of technology, though there aren't so many materials on it, is www.iste.org/.

COMPUTER SOFTWARE

Software is so much improved that we can find material in virtually every subject and at every grade or capability level. However, people in every business try to sell products, and very often, material that you find in educational information that looks as if it might be valuable is not acceptable for your class. You will want to look carefully at software before you purchase it for classroom use. If you buy materials that are too easy for your class or too juvenile, you will have wasted money because middle and secondary students are very sensitive to having someone (or some software) talk down to them. If you can find materials that are aimed more directly at interaction with the student instead of tutorial or drill, students will more likely enjoy and use the product (Ornstein, 1990). If a company has a product that you think you could use, if they are not willing to allow you to try it out or come to demonstrate it to you, you can probably find another piece of software in which to invest that will be just as good. You want to avoid buying software that doesn't meet the needs of your students. If you aren't careful, you may have piles of useless computer software stacked in your storage room next to the film-strips and 16 or 35 mm movies of the previous century.

TELEVISION, VIDEOS, AND AUDIOTAPES

Television has come such a long way since teachers first began using it in the classroom. It is wonderful to be able to use some of the cable channels that are for educational purposes. There are several networks that prepare materials just for the classroom with exercises, question, discussion-time suggestions, and good current-event or historical narratives. Some schools have a channel that all of the classes watch at one time because that channel broadcasts special programs geared toward the objectives mandated by the state. Many students study current events by watching some of the news channels. Young people are so tuned in to commercial television that the transition to a learning channel will not be difficult for them. It is advantageous for you to know in advance what the channel is going to air and have a study guide for it. Such items are available for the asking, and most of the channels have either an e-mail address or a free telephone number for you to call to arrange to get materials. Many of the channels have videotapes and DVDs of their programming so that if you decide that a program would be worth watching in your content classroom, you could order the videotape for a nominal purchase price. Using current videos gives each teacher something on which to hang the class discussion and a way to involve students through the use of a familiar medium. The public access televisions station will also have some special educational offerings that will not cost you to use in your individual classrooms. They will also have a Web address to visit about such materials.

Commercial films offer good teaching situations if you can use them in connection with the reading that you are doing in class. A play using Shakespearean English, for instance, is so much more vivid if the students watch part of it in a filmed version. A teacher must be very careful, however, that she does not violate copyright laws when showing rented films to a class. It is best to check this out by looking up copyright conditions on the Internet. The laws concerning copyright change from time to time, and items that may be all right today may need some adjusting before you elect to show a film next year. You can also check it out with the United States Copyright office via e-mail. Explain exactly what your plan is, and they will let you know if your plan has a problem.

One interesting assignment that you might consider design-ing in order to have your students use a video is to have them write their "reader's theater" version of a script then perform it and videotape it for others in the class to see. That would give double value to that kind of video technology. You can generally find the particulars for creating a reader's theater script by looking under that title on the Internet. You may even find reader's theater scripts available for downloading if the work has already been done for classroom purposes.

WORD PROCESSING

One thing that you certainly will want to do is to encourage the students in your classes to use word processing software to create written assignments. In using word processing, they are developing their skills well, but they are also giving you material that you are more likely to be able to read. Text well written in manuscript is good, but text well written in type makes assignments so much easier for you to mark. Some things, like journal assignments, are better written by hand so that you know that a student has done her own writing, but you and the student can learn much by using the technology of word processing. If you suggest word processing assignments, that is all right, but you have to use caution in saying that you require the assignment be typed using word processing software. Remember many students do not have such equipment available at home, and they just won't have access to such tools. Even giving extra points for assignments using word processors is unfair if all students do not have access to this technology.

OVERHEAD TRANSPARENCIES

One frequent task you might have had to do at the university where you recently graduated might have been to make sets of overhead transparencies. Though there are still myriad uses for transparencies, the PowerPoint-type projection on the screen of a television monitor has rapidly taken over that area, making transparency usage somewhat outmoded. For math and science classes where problems are worked on the transparencies, that approach still seems viable. But when you think of how much better you can represent a cell using computer presentations with slides and interaction, then you don't want to waste much time with an overhead transparency if the technology for a PowerPoint-type presentation is available. These kinds of presentations may be just as easily copied for distribution as can the transparency. Often the Power-Point slides, being typed on a computer, are more accurate and readable than handmade transparencies used on an overhead.

TECHNOLOGICAL CHANGES

Technological advances are made so quickly in this postmodern time that it is difficult to keep abreast of the latest gadget or learning tool. Try to keep up with the materials that are available to your school. One school represented on one Web location had a story that its district was spending $100,000 each year on computer software. The district had also dedicated $1.5 million from the operating budgets to have computers on the students' desks. Such availability would be fantastic, but you may be relegated to what is available in your media center or library. When you look into what is available, if it sounds useful, check it out. Software is certainly one area in which a teacher cannot always stay ahead.

If you feel inadequate to teach or to use such technological materials in your classroom, buy one of the current books that will enhance your capabilities. They are easy to follow, and if you take just a little time to learn the proper way to use technology, you will be a much more effective teacher. Your students will fare better when they are compared with others who have not had this kind of teaching. If you can apply technology, it also lets your students know that you are a lifelong learner; it is a good way for you to model learning new skills. Again, remember to give yourself time to learn how to use technology effectively. If you don't enter the classroom technology-literate, begin implementing technology a little at a time—whatever you can master comfortably. Also remember that your students may be far more advanced than you are. It may be possible for you to identify one or two reliable students who can become your technology assistants. As with to mastering assessments, as your technology expertise grows, you will be comfortable using it more.

JOURNAL TOPICS

- How do you think technology will be changing in the near future for the improvement of education?
- Plan a PowerPoint presentation that you can use to teach one of your classes in a few days, showing what slides you would design for that production.
- Review at least one piece of software compatible with your classroom content area and critique its value to you as a new teacher.

CHAPTER SEVEN

Making Parent Communication Work

C ommunicating with parents is both rewarding and frustrating. With so much to do to prepare to teach and deal with students in the classroom, it would be easy for a teacher to ignore parent communication. However, the teacher who takes time to develop lines of communication and ways to keep those lines open to parents has tapped a source that can help him become an effective teacher.

There is a wide range of parental involvement at the secondary level. Parents of students in kindergarten through sixth grade are much more likely to come to parent-teacher conferences and open-house nights sponsored by the district. The older the child, the less parents are involved in their children's academic lives. Year after year, most school districts host an open house early in the semester. All schools in the district participate. Elementary teachers complain that they never have enough time to visit with all the parents who attend. Middle school teachers declare that the evening is a success—just enough time to visit with all the parents who attend. High school teachers complain that the evening is a waste of time; only a handful of parents attend, and these are the parents of the students who already perform at high levels.

There are many reasons for the smaller amount of participation from parents of older students. Because these students are growing into young adulthood, many parents feel that they should not be as active in their children's school lives unless problems are developing. At the same time, older students are not as excited about their parents meeting their teachers as they were when they were younger. They no longer have one principal teacher but may have as many as seven different teachers. The ties to teachers are not as strong as they were in elementary school when the school day centered around one specific teacher. Older students are also pushing for independence, and having their parents show up at school may smack of childishness. However, even though they shy away from visiting their children's teachers, most parents want to know how their children are doing in school, and they appreciate a teacher's efforts to keep them informed.

MAKING TIME FOR COMMUNICATION

Early in the school year, you should develop a plan for informing parents and laying a foundation for two-way communication. You might begin by mailing parents or guardians a brief overview of what you hope to accomplish for the semester, a list of your classroom rules, and an invitation for parents to call you—at school—if they have questions.

Plan this first communication carefully. Be sure that your letter is brief, certainly no longer than one page. Keep in mind that if every teacher sent home a letter, the parents would have five to seven letters to read that evening for every child they have. You need to be succinct, friendly yet professional, and accurate. Proofread your text carefully. A letter filled with spelling, grammar, and typographical errors will certainly not create a favorable impression. You might want to include a tear-away section at the bottom of the page for parents or guardians to sign so that the student can return the statement the next day and earn a few extra points. Giving extra points is usually a good way to motivate students to follow through on your request for delivering information to their parents. And even though all of your secondary students will not take letters home or return the form (or, heaven forbid, forge their parents' signatures), when it's time for a parent-teacher conference, evidence that you have tried to communicate with parents shows your interest in your students' and their parents' participation.

With the increasing use of technology, school districts and individual teachers may have Web sites. This is both good and bad. Using these sites is an efficient way to disseminate information, but it takes time to keep them updated. If you are not required to use a Web site, it might be wise to wait until your second or third year to experiment with such an instrument. During the first years, you don't want to be tied to something that becomes a burden. However, as soon as you are able to take advantage of Web sites, you will find it both challenging and enjoyable to keep your students and their parents informed via the Internet.

PLAN FOR POSITIVE COMMUNICATION

Although the secondary teacher's class load is much larger than that of an elementary teacher, secondary teachers need to spend time sharing student success with parents. Composing short "good for you" notes, writing remarks on sticky notes, and suggesting that students share them with their parents is a good way to encourage students and inform parents of student successes. It is possible to find something positive about every student:

Don, thanks for listening in class today.

Kay, your idea for an essay topic was interesting and creative.

Les, your sense of humor always makes me smile.

Kia, thanks for helping another student understand the assignment.

Doing a few of these each week, starting with students who are struggling and ending with students who do well in your class, makes this a workable suggestion. You will be surprised at how many of your students share the notes with their parents and at how appreciative parents are of receiving good news. Also, if you offer words of encouragement early in the grading period to students who struggle and you later have to send deficiency or failing notices, the parents have a sense of balance. Their child needs to do better, and you have notified them of that fact, but you are more than just a bearer of bad news. You care about their child's successes as well as her problems. Never give artificial compliments. Your students will know you are not sincere. However, recognizing even small achievements often gives students a sense of worth.

MAKING YOURSELF AVAILABLE

If you want to communicate effectively with parents, you must make yourself available. There is a fine line between being available and being taken advantage of, so you need to know what kind of parental relationship you want to develop. When at all possible, plan for communication to take place at school. It is difficult for you to remember all the details of a student's work or problems once you are at home. Marian told of parental involvement:

One of my survival techniques was, as much as possible, to keep school issues at school. After several years of unproductive evening conversations with parents, I stopped taking my grade book home with me. I had discovered that once I left the school, the details of a student's work became muddled by my "outside of school" life. If a parent called to discuss her child's work, I asked if I could call her from school the next day because all of my records were there. Not only did that help me refocus information in the context where it occurred, it gave me some time to think about the situation and plan what I wanted to discuss with the parent.

Since much of my teaching experience was in a rural area, I knew many of my students' parents. I found it uncomfortable (and sometimes unpleasant) to discuss students at ball games, in the grocery store, or at church. I began asking the parents to call the school secretary to set up a time for a conference so that I could show them student work and student grades. I found this to work well for two reasons. First, it gave me an opportunity to think through the parents' concerns and plan the appropriate response to their request for information or help. Second, it kept me from giving misinformation. Once

I was away from school, it was hard to remember everything
that had happened that day or that week. If the student
had failed to turn in work, or possibly scored low on a test,
I couldn't always remember. It was much easier to ask the
parent to set up a conference than to have to call the next week
and begin a conversation with "I told you Jay was doing well in
class, but I didn't realize at the time that she hadn't turned in
her last assignment."

MAKING PARENT AND TEACHER EXPECTATIONS MESH

Parents seem to be divided into four groups when it comes to
expectations for their children: Those who agree with and support
a teacher's expectations; those who are willing to settle for less
than what the student is capable of; those who have unrealistically high expectations; and those not involved in their children's
education at all. The first group is easy to work with, as they agree
with the teacher's expectations and support the teacher's efforts
to motivate and inspire the students. The second group seems
willing to settle for less than the students' best. Parents in this
group have the attitude of "I didn't do so well in school, and I'm
making it okay, so why should my kids expect to do any better?"
Sometimes a teacher can persuade this type of parent to join in
her efforts to encourage the child, and sometimes the teacher has
to maintain a higher standard in spite of the parent's expectations. As long as the teacher doesn't say or do anything to indicate
a lack of respect for the parents, students often respond to the
teacher's encouragement and set higher goals for themselves.

One of the most difficult tensions to resolve is that of the third
group of parents—those who have unrealistically high expectations for their children. Quite often this group consists of parents
who have done well in school or in a career who want their
children to succeed as well. However, the group can also consist of
parents who didn't do well in school or a career but who want
their children to do better than they did.

Working with parents who have unrealistic expectations can
be a challenging situation. You must be very diplomatic as you
explain how the child is functioning in your class and why she is

not able to meet the parents' expectations. You never want to destroy the hope that a child can do better, but you also don't want to destroy a child's ego as she overachieves and still fails to meet her parents' goals. You must work to form a positive relationship with the parents and student and discuss ways you can work as a team to meet the needs of that student. Try to find ways to inspire her to stretch to her full potential. You could suggest tutoring, or you could suggest dividing difficult assignments into smaller segments so that the task is less overwhelming. You might also want to confer with the special education teacher to find out what strategies would be helpful to a struggling student, or consult with the school counselor to find out ways to help the student. It is possible that in some circumstances, the school counselor is your best source of help. He will have the expertise to work with the emotional needs of both the parents and the student.

The fourth group of parents is composed of people who, for whatever reason, choose not to be involved in their children's education. This can be disheartening for a teacher, especially if the children have given up on themselves. That is when it is important for a teacher to realize that he may be the most encouraging person in a child's life. He must refuse to give up on the student and look for ways to encourage him to do his best. The rewards are great for the teacher who is able to help that student reach beyond his environment and experience success.

One group of students needs to be mentioned at this point—emancipated students. These are students who do not live with either parents or guardians. These students have left home and are living with the parents of a friend, living with a boyfriend or girlfriend, living with a relative who is not designated as a guardian, or living alone. Older emancipated students are often working to provide for themselves as well as attending school. When you find out that you have an emancipated student, you should first inform the principal or counselor. You need to initiate whatever procedure the school has for checking on these students to see that they are in a safe environment. If the environment is safe, then try to communicate with the adult in the home just as you would the student's parents. Check with your principal to see what to do about matters that require parental signatures, then follow his instructions carefully. Usually, if the student is 18 or older, the student is permitted to sign her own legal documents.

However, taking that student on a field trip that requires permission may need to be handled in a different manner. Your principal will know what you should do.

MAKING PARENT-TEACHER CONFERENCES PLEASANT

One of the most potentially stressful situations for teachers and parents is the parent-teacher conference. One of the main reasons for stress is the assumption that something is wrong. If a parent calls to schedule a conference, the first thing a teacher is likely to do is to wonder what she has done that would cause the parent to want to talk to her. If the teacher calls to schedule a conference, the parent wonders what her child has done to cause trouble. A teacher sometimes better understands this situation after her own children become old enough for a teacher to call *her* to set up a conference. At that point she can experience the worry and anxiety that parents often experience, and perhaps better understand how defensive a parent can become when frustrated or upset. Such experiences make a good surviving teacher realize the need for parents and teachers to work together to reach positive solutions.

If at all possible, schedule the conference during school hours. If that is not an option, try to schedule the conference either before or after the school day but at a time when an administrator is still in the building. Most conferences turn out to be pleasant, but just in case you run into problems, it is important to have another person in the building who can help you reach a solution or terminate the conference. It also helps keep both parties from making statements they regret. As a new teacher, it would be an opportunity to gain advice about how you handled the situation. For that reason, instead of the principal, you might want to enlist your mentor or a teacher with whom you have shared questions about what to expect in the conference.

The first thing you want to do is to put the parents at ease. Many parents have unpleasant school memories of conferences or confrontations with teachers. You should greet parents and make them feel comfortable in your environment. Rather than sit behind your desk, pull desks together so that you and the parents can sit side by side. That gives an unstated message of partnership, of working together for the good of the student. Have the student's file and a copy of her grades. Remember the confidentiality issues we discussed in Chapter 3, and be careful to protect the confidentiality of your other students.

After inviting the parents to be seated, thank them for coming. You can do this in all good conscience—even if you are going to discuss behavior issues of a student who has made you really angry—if you remember that for parents to agree to a conference is an indication that they truly care about the welfare of their child. That is something that should always be commended. As you discuss issues with parents, avoid using educational jargon. Sometimes it is tempting to "put a parent in his place," and you can do that extremely well by using "educationese." If you do, however, you run the risk of immediately alienating the parent, because he will consciously or subconsciously see these as attempts to belittle him.

If you have called the conference, begin with a clear statement of the problem. Try to phrase your introduction in an objective way. For example, if you called the conference because Sherry has been harassing another student, you could begin by saying, "Thank you for coming today. I'd like to talk to you about some things I've seen Sherry doing that could cause problems for her as well as for other students." You must be honest but not judgmental as you explain what you have seen:

> On two occasions I've had to ask Sherry to stop teasing or poking one of the girls who sits across the aisle from her. The girl responds in a way that lets me know that she doesn't think Sherry is being friendly or funny. I've talked with both of the girls, and Sherry doesn't seem to understand that her actions could be seen as a form of harassment (or maybe Sherry seems unconcerned that her actions could be seen as a form of harassment). Has this been a problem for Sherry before?

At this point, if the parents say they have had this problem before, you could ask them how they handled it in the past. If they have never had the problem before, ask what kinds of things they could recommend that they think might work in helping Sherry stop the destructive behavior.

Efforts to involve parents in the solution to a problem are usually well received. Most parents want their children to be successful and fair to others. Sometimes they have given the teacher good advice concerning effective things they have done with their child. Often they are surprised by the behavior of their child and want to know what the teacher would suggest. Usually, working together the teacher and the parents can propose a solution to the problem.

There have been conferences in which the suggestions of the parents have been totally unacceptable. In such cases, the teacher must explain why she doesn't think the parents' suggestions will work—maybe she has already tried what they suggested, maybe their suggestion is too severe for the situation, maybe they are too defensive and insist that the problem is not with their child. Before the conference, a teacher should always prepare solutions that she thinks might work, and when she can't accept the suggestions of the parents, she can tell them what she would like to try and then ask for their cooperation. Many times the parents are relieved that the teacher has suggestions because they themselves aren't sure what will and will not work.

MAKING THE BEST
OF A BAD SITUATION

Although most parent-teacher conferences end pleasantly and have positive results, there is the occasional conference that feels like failure. In these extreme cases, you must minimize the damage and move to the next level. If parents become belligerent, you need to end the conference as quickly as possible. You don't want to panic even though nervousness is part of the scenario, so before you have that first conference, think through what you could do if you sense that any conference is moving in an uncomfortable direction. If possible, ask the parents to consult the principal with you. You can make the request by stating something like, "It seems that we may not be able to agree (or continue). Would you come with me to the principal's office and let's see what we can work out." Then leave the room as if you expect them to follow. If they follow, fine. If they don't, continue to the principal's office, tell her what has happened, and ask for her help.

If you realize that the conference is moving in a direction with which you are uncomfortable and there is no one in the principal's office, tell the parents that you would like to ask the principal to schedule a conference with you and them. Again, if they become belligerent, gather your things and leave the room. Leave the building and find a security officer or go home and call your principal. This is not a cowardly way to handle the situation at all. If you feel threatened in any way, you have every right to call off the conference and ask for help. As soon as you are calm, write down an accurate account of the conference. Be sure to include sentences that describe the behavior that made you feel threatened. Keep a copy in the file you have for the parents' child and give another copy to your principal. Remember that this scenario is certainly the exception. However, just as you need to have a plan for dealing with classroom crises (Chapter 3), you need to have a plan for dealing with an unsuccessful parent-teacher conference.

MAKING ADJUSTMENTS FOR COMMUNICATION ABOUT SPECIAL NEEDS STUDENTS

In many schools, the regular classroom teacher is called into conferences for special needs students. In those meetings, the special education teacher serves as moderator to facilitate communication. There are times, such as open house or parent-teacher conference days, when parents of special needs students may want to visit with the classroom teacher. If at all possible, ask the special education specialist to be present. His knowledge of the student's abilities and federal regulations will be valuable as you and the parents discuss student progress and your expectations.

If you are in an area that has second language learners, you needn't be fearful of parental conferences with non-English-speaking parents. Ask your principal or counselor for help in finding a person in the community who can act as an interpreter. Then encourage parents of these students to attend conferences and participate in activities the same as you would English-speaking parents. Many cultural and emotional barriers could be lowered if all parents felt the school personnel were approachable.

MAKING TELEPHONE
CONFERENCES EFFECTIVE

Although face-to-face conferences give you a better chance to read a parent's body language, telephone conferences are sometimes your only way to discuss issues with parents. If school-day conferences are entirely out of the question, call the parent and set a definite date and time for the conference outside the school day. That gives you time to gather the student's file and your grade book so that you will have the information you need to share with the parent. Conduct your conference just as you would if the parent were present: that is, thank the parent for taking time to talk with you, state the problem clearly, don't use educational jargon, and so forth.

As with face-to-face conferences, most discussions conclude pleasantly, and you and the parent have a better understanding of the problem as well as possible solutions. Also, just as with face-to-face conferences, there will occasionally be the extreme telephone conversation that deteriorates into an unpleasant experience. Remember that just because you can't see the person on the other end of the line doesn't mean that you have to accept rude behavior. If the parent becomes belligerent or abusive, simply say that you will be glad to schedule a conference with the parent and the principal and hang up. Again, document the conversation, put a copy in the student's folder and give a copy to your principal. If the parent makes any threats to you, contact the police department as well. You may or may not want your students and their parents to have access to your private telephone number. In the past, that was seldom a problem. However, in a world where technology makes everyone more vulnerable, you may want to consider making calls to parents from school telephones rather than your cell or land line.

MAKING PARENTS AWARE
OF FAILING GRADES

It is a common practice for schools to send deficiency or failure notices to parents of students who are failing classes. Unfortunately, sometimes these are sent so late in the grading period that by the time the parents learn of the students' poor grades, the students don't have enough time to correct the problem. It will benefit your students if you send out failure notices at the end of the first third of the grading period as well as in the middle of the grading period. Because most schools require that you provide a weekly list of students who might be ineligible for competitive activities, it will only take a little additional time for you to send an extra notice, and that notice might be just the thing that motivates a student to work a little harder to pass. Keep a copy in your files so that if the notices don't make it home, you have evidence that you did make an attempt to notify the parents.

MAKING STUDENTS AND PARENTS RESPONSIBLE

Occasionally, a student's parent will request that a teacher notify him if the student's grades drop below a certain level. Sometimes that level is an F, but sometimes a parent requests notification if the student's grades drop below a C, B, or even an A. Parents may also request that the teacher notify them if students fail to turn in assignments or remind them when major assignments are due. Either request is unacceptable. Although both seem like well-intentioned requests, they spell trouble for the teacher. The problem for the teacher is that if he fails to notify the parents (maybe he forgot, maybe he called and the parents weren't home, maybe he didn't have time to call because of other responsibilities), the teacher runs the risk, in the eyes of the parent, of assuming the responsibility for the student's lower performance.

The best way to avoid this problem is to avoid taking the responsibility for notifying parents. Instead, put the responsibility back on the student and his parents. For example, if parents want to be notified of assignment deadlines, tell them that their child is welcome to pick up an extra syllabus to give to them. If the parents want a weekly account of their child's grades, ask them to call you each Friday afternoon before school dismisses. If their concern is whether or not their child is eligible for competition, check with your principal to see if they can call the school office and ask the secretary for the information. Their wanting to keep check on their child's progress is good. Their wanting you to assume the responsibility for notifying them specifically is not good. If you can't do it for all of your students, you can't do it for one or just a few. Parents who truly want to know the status of their child's assignment deadlines or their child's grades will be willing to assume the responsibility for acquiring that information.

MAKING PARENT COMMUNICATION A POSITIVE EXPERIENCE

In conclusion, teachers are usually rewarded for their efforts to communicate with parents. If you can remember that your goal in talking with parents is to help their children succeed in your class, you will realize that the occasional unpleasant experience is over-shadowed by the positive conferences you have. Both parents and students will appreciate your sincerity and your willingness to make the extra effort to communicate with them. They will share their positive experiences with other parents in the community, and you will establish a reputation as a teacher who truly cares about his students. That in itself is a huge reward.

JOURNAL TOPICS

- Imagine a conference with the parents of a student who is failing your class. What are some ways you could explain the problem? What would be some suggestions you might make for the parents to become involved in the solution?
- Imagine a conference with parents of a student who is misbehaving in class. How could you state the problem? What kinds of things could you ask the parents to do to solve the problem?
- Imagine a conference in which a parent becomes belliger-ent. How would you contact your principal if she had already left the building? What telephone numbers would you need to have available?

C H A P T E R   E I G H T

Making Yourself a Professional

Teaching is one of the most rewarding professions. Teachers have the opportunity to make positive contributions to the lives of children, and those contributions will live on long after the teacher has left the profession. As you will soon discover, there are two elements to becoming a successful educator: the process of becoming a teacher and the process of becoming a professional. Both processes start with student teaching and continue until retirement. It is a process of putting what you have learned into practice and then continuing to learn. It is also one of the rewarding aspects of teaching—there is always something to learn or improve. There are three components to becoming a professional that merit consideration: attitudes, actions, and associations.

DEVELOPING THE ATTITUDE OF A PROFESSIONAL

A basic attitude on which others build is an attitude of respect. You must have respect for your students, your administrators, your colleagues, and yourself. You must give respect and expect respect. It is easy for a teacher to be overwhelmed with the enormous task of teaching and to doubt his effectiveness. Think about what you have accomplished in order to stand in front of a classroom. You have completed 4 years of training and proven yourself as a student, and you have passed certification tests that qualify you, in the eyes of the state departments of education, to be in the classroom. You have survived application and interview processes and have become the district's choice to work with its children. It's true that you may be nervous about what you are required to do and how you will do it, but you have not entered the classroom unprepared or unqualified. You deserve your own respect.

You may not always want to respect all of your colleagues, but giving them respect is as important as respecting yourself. There will be teachers who are the epitome of the professional educator. It will be easy for you to admire and respect them. There will also be an occasional teacher who seems to reside at the bottom of the professional scale. You may be tempted to allow your students to engage in negative talk about that person, and you may be tempted to agree with them. That would be unacceptable. For one thing, students are fickle, and the teacher who chimes in with the students' negative talk about one of her colleagues one day may be the topic of the students' negative talk the next day. More important, as a professional, you must insist on students' respecting the profession of teaching. Help them to realize that unless you can get inside the life of another person (an obvious impossibility), it is impossible to know why people act and react the way they do. If you insist that everyone be treated with respect in your classroom, you need to insist that every teacher or administrator in your district receive respect as well. Expectations for your students' classroom behavior extend to the entire system. You will have many opportunities to model this behavior for your students.

Treating your administrators with respect seems like an obvious point that should need no discussion, but many educators find themselves in conflict with administrators by becoming involved in other teachers' battles. You must be extremely careful, especially in the first years in a district, to stay out of conflicts that have been brewing before you were hired. Be suspicious of teachers who befriend you by sharing negative comments about administrators and faculty members. Don't engage in negative conversations with them, and refuse any offers to join with them in their plans to solve the problems. That will spell disaster for your credibility and career. As you mature in the profession, you will develop an understanding of what battles should be fought so that the quality of education will improve. Those are the conflicts that deserve your attention. However, conflicts between faculty and administration based on differences in personality or differences in philosophies are conflicts you want to avoid.

You must respect your students if you are to be an effective teacher. You will find it amusing in the future to return to school before the new term starts and hear some of your colleagues complain that teaching would be a great profession if it weren't for the students they have to endure. A good way to remind yourself of why you have entered the teaching profession is to greet each class on the first day of school with, "I'm so glad you're here today. Without you, I wouldn't be needed!"

Respect for students is at the heart of our profession. Teachers must respect students for their individual differences. Instead of becoming frustrated because of a need to plan for so much divergence, teachers need to look for ways to help students celebrate their differences and those of their classmates. Students who are struggling need to know that teachers respect their efforts and will do their part to help the students succeed. Students who do well and learn easily need to know that teachers respect their abilities (which sometimes surpass the teachers' own) and want to help them stretch as far as they can. Students who can't learn at the moment because of the problems they bring with them to school—abuse, neglect, poverty, and despair—need to know that their teachers respect them and their struggles and that they want to help their students as much as they can. Students are masters of observation. If a teacher truly respects them, they will know. As teachers offer respect to students, those students will offer their respect to their teachers.

AN ATTITUDE OF HOPE

An effective teacher is realistically optimistic. That means that even though there are sometimes difficulties with students, parents, colleagues, administrators, or special people in his or her life outside of school, an effective teacher is able to look through the problems and see hope on the other side. Sometimes it takes a conscious effort to be able to do this. Teaching is like rearing children. It is impossible to be certain that you have done a good job until it is too late to make changes. However, if you stay in the profession long enough, you will begin to see the fruit of your labor. You will see your former students doing well in other classes, finding satisfying careers, getting married, and beginning families of their own. You will also see many who make life-changing mistakes, but who accept the responsibility for their mistakes and become mature adults. Experience will give you the ability to develop and nurture that realistic optimism.

You also have to nurture realistic optimism about yourself and your profession. From the beginning of your career, look for ways to broaden your teaching base. People in virtually every profession become discouraged and burn out, but those who become disgruntled in the field of education are a dangerous liability because of the damage they can do to students who become the focus of their dissatisfaction. You can avoid burnout if you look for ways to explore new areas of education. Perhaps you could get a second endorsement in a related field so that you can change subject areas for a while. Maybe you need to request a different grade level for a year or two. Sometimes moving to another building or a different district provides the change needed for renewing that love of teaching. Under the most extreme circumstances, maybe considering a different profession is the right thing to do. The point is, if you realize that you are not enjoying your job, try to make changes that will renew your interest in teaching.

ACTING AS A PROFESSIONAL

It seems that members of no other profession are under such constant and close scrutiny as are teachers. That makes sense if you remember that teachers are charged with the responsibility of molding a precious commodity—our children. During your student teaching and sometimes during the first year of teaching, you have not been completely on your own. Another person—a supervising teacher or assigned mentor—has been partially responsible for your actions. Once you have completed that period of supervision, finally, you alone are responsible for your actions. Teachers have a great deal of autonomy that is not present in other professions. This gives us opportunity to be creative and to test our theories of teaching and learning. We go into our classrooms, shut the door, and conduct class—many times with no interaction with other professionals for most of the school day. That autonomy brings with it a degree of freedom and an additional level of responsibility. Because teachers are not closely supervised, they must make sure that they plan carefully and use good judgment because they are accountable for what happens in their classrooms and how they respond to the responsibilities assigned to them.

Because of our autonomy, new teachers may feel that they must operate alone, without "bothering" another teacher with his problems and concerns. That is a misconception. Many experienced teachers are glad to answer questions and offer suggestions as long as you shoulder your part of the responsibility and don't infringe needlessly on their time. There are also educational Web sites (such as the National Council of Teachers of English site) that have ongoing discussion forums for teachers—new and experienced—that could have information pertaining to your specific questions or problems.

ATTENDING TO EXTRA DUTY

You may have been surprised at how many additional duties you have been assigned. The smaller the school district, the heavier the list of extra assignments. You may have to give up part of your lunch or planning period to supervise students. You may have to arrive early and stay late to supervise students who are on the school grounds before and after school. You may have to sponsor a student organization or help another teacher plan and sponsor an activity. Sometimes you are paid for the extra time you spend on these activities, but usually, they are just added to your teaching duties as part of the job.

Do not take these extra duty assignments lightly. You must always remember that if you are assigned extra duty, you are responsible for what happens during your assignment whether you are physically present or not. For example, if you are on bus duty and a student misbehaves and causes injury to school property or another student, if you have made a reasonable effort to stop the destructive behavior, your efforts will be supported by your administrator, even if the situation became serious. If, however, you were assigned bus duty at the end of the day, and you forgot and failed to show up, you may be held responsible for the situation, and such negligence of responsibility may put your job in jeopardy. That makes it imperative that you be prompt and present. Check your daily calendar and plan ahead to keep up with those duties that may otherwise slip up on you.

Invariably, there will be someone on your faculty who never completes extra duty assignments. She always forgets, shows up late, or simply refuses to do the assignments. Even though it seems that she is never reprimanded for these lapses, remember that she is taking a very great personal and professional risk. Don't let her apparent ability to avoid part of her duties tempt you to follow her example. Her lack of responsibility is an invitation for trouble that could even extend, in extreme cases, to lawsuits.

AVOIDING COMPROMISING SITUATIONS

You must always think ahead to consequences your actions could have. A very sensitive situation is privately conferencing with students. Even though there are times when you need to speak privately with a student, you should try to do it in as public a manner as possible, especially if the student is of the opposite sex. Leave your classroom door open and stand or sit where you are visible from outside the room, but far enough inside so that people outside the door can't hear you. Avoid touching the student, even if you intend your touch to be a form of encouragement such as a pat on the back, a quick hug, or a grip on the shoulder or arm to show your support. Conduct student conferences during the school day, if at all possible, not before or after school when teachers and students have left the building. If you think that the student you are conferencing is at all romantically interested in you (and that happens more frequently than you can imagine) or is flattered by your attention, conduct conferences with that student only in the presence of other colleagues—another teacher, the principal, or the counselor. There are so many accounts of teachers "behaving improperly" with students that it is best to err on the side of being too cautious rather than creating a situation that could be compromising for you in any way. Your career is at risk by any such improper suggestion, even if nothing improper was intended.

RESPONDING TO STUDENT
TELEPHONE CALLS AND NOTES

Because telephone calls and notes require more private responses, you need to be wary of situations that could, again, compromise you. If you receive an inappropriate telephone call, hang up immediately, document the incident, and report the call to your principal. If you think you recognize the student's voice, make a note of who you think it is. If the student introduces himself, note his name. If you receive an inappropriate note from a student, do the same thing, except give the principal a copy of the note and keep the original—in a safe place. Never take these incidents lightly, and don't ignore them. As we have seen from news reports, students sometimes create elaborate fantasies that can lead to real or imagined encounters with teachers. Don't become paranoid over such possibilities, but be aware of any actions that indicate a student is becoming attached to you in a way that could be unsafe or unhealthy for either of you.

LIVING IN A "GLASS HOUSE"

Teachers deserve the right to have a life outside the school setting. They deserve the right to participate in any lifestyle they choose and to socialize wherever and with whomever they choose. Unfortunately, the smaller the community you live in, the less freedom you have to live any way you want. By law you have these rights, but from a practical standpoint, parents often expect teachers to forgo their rights if the parents see the teacher as having a negative or threatening influence on their children. You need to consider carefully the mores and standards of the community in which you teach. If you are uncomfortable with the expectations the community has for you, perhaps you need to decide whether you want to insist upon your constitutional rights to your private lifestyle or perhaps find another community where you are more autonomous and totally free to live the way you want. You may decide that being yourself and living the way you choose is a moral issue you want the community to address. If that is the case, you should be willing to do what your conscience dictates, realizing that the battle you may face could be extremely difficult. No matter how well you are liked or received, there is no way to know in advance whether or not you will have the support from administrators and colleagues that you want or need. Weigh the costs carefully and then proceed to do what you feel is important.

ACCEPTING THE CHALLENGE
OF LIFELONG LEARNING

It is both amusing and annoying when people in the community say things such as, "Teaching must be nice. You have all that time off in the summer." What a misconception! It's true that there are teachers who avoid the classroom during the summer vacation. Some of them have family responsibilities that require their intense involvement during summer months, especially if they are single parents or have young children. Some of them have to find a summer job to bring in extra income. Some of them really need time off to rest or schedule medical procedures that would require days or weeks of recuperation. However, eventually, the effective teacher realizes that to stay abreast of new developments in teaching and learning theory, she must enter the summer classroom. Continuing your education will help you grow professionally as you learn things that will translate into good classroom practice.

Becoming a student yourself also helps you maintain the student perspective. Any veteran teacher can think of times when her experiences as a student helped her better understand what students experienced in her classroom. For example, Joyce had one professor who had the annoying characteristic of making an assignment without first considering and verbalizing exactly what outcome he expected for the assignment. Having had that frustrating experience helped Joyce look at the assignments she made and ask herself if the criteria for assessments were clear and well designed. Another professor assigned his class to become members of cooperative learning groups, and his students, who were secondary school teachers, learned that allowing a few minutes for the group to socialize before beginning the assigned task was an important part of the group dynamics of cooperative learning. When those teachers used cooperative learning groups in their own classrooms, they intentionally built in time for the students to socialize as a component of the cooperative learning experience. Many teachers find that as they continue their education, in almost every class or workshop they take, they are constantly thinking, "How can we use the various professors' classroom techniques to advantage in our own classrooms?"

Financing additional education can sometimes be a challenge. It is ironic that, for the most part, the education profession does not often provide funding for teachers to engage in professional development. Many corporations absorb the cost of any additional training their employees must have—most schools do not. It is possible to find workshops and seminars that are offered at a nominal cost. Some of these are funded by organizations that provide stipends or scholarships for participants, and some of them are provided by the school district at no cost. Fortunately for some teachers, there are schools that provide stipends for professional development activities from money the district receives from state and federal agencies. There are foundations that offer financial assistance to educators who participate in professional development activities that the foundations fund or approve. It is also possible for a teacher to receive grant funding for other types of training or college courses. Although it may take a little creative imagination or a little research, often educators can find professional development activities that will help them grow as professionals, as well as find some sources of funding that will enable them to participate in such activities.

ASSOCIATING WITH PROFESSIONALS

Membership in your discipline's professional organizations is an important component in becoming a professional. There are such organizations in almost every discipline: for example, the American Library Association, International Reading Association, International Technology Educational Association, Music Educators National Conference, National Art Education, National Association for Sport and Physical Education, National Council for the Social Studies, National Council of Teachers of English, National Council of Teachers of Mathematics, National Science Teachers Association, and Teachers of Psychology in Secondary Schools. These groups publish journals that provide information on current research, theory, and practice. They also provide excellent convention experiences and professional development opportunities. It is so easy for a teacher to become trapped within the walls of her classroom and have no concept of the big picture and how her job fits into the profession as a whole. By becoming affiliated with the larger professional organizations, she can maintain a focus on the big picture and compare what she sees and experiences in her classroom with what other educators are seeing and experiencing. I always found it encouraging and invigorating to read the journals and attend the professional meetings. There were always groups of teachers who were willing to talk about their students and classrooms. Engaging in dialogue with them gives a teacher self-confidence as she sees her practice mirrored in other professionals' stories, recognizing the issues that cause them concern, and realizing that her experiences were as authentic and important as theirs were.

ALLOWING TIME FOR PROFESSIONAL GROWTH

Becoming a professional in your eyes and the eyes of your colleagues takes time. You begin by realizing that your training in education has prepared you to assume the role of a professional educator. Year after year, you build on that preparation as you develop expertise in teaching and in dealing with students, parents, and other teachers. You create a reputation for yourself based on your actions and reactions.

You may experience an occasional setback as you disappoint yourself by not handling a student or situation in a way satisfying to you, but the longer you teach and strive for excellence, the more comfortable you will feel with your professional persona. Teaching is a constantly evolving profession that requires optimism and growth. As you examine your career, learn to look mostly at the successes and celebrate them. You must also learn to look at mistakes and evaluate them. By maintaining a positive outlook and engaging in such learning experiences, you will become a professional who enjoys her work and who can share that enjoyment with her students.

NURTURING YOURSELF

Teachers are generous people—generous with their time, their interest, and their concern. Often they give so much of themselves that they deplete their physical and emotional reserves. For that reason, it is critical that you begin your career by building in intentional time for yourself. You need to eat well, exercise, and play. There will be many days, and sometimes weeks, when the demands of teaching are heavy. Testing preparation seems to threaten the sanity of everyone in the profession. Realize that you must meet your responsibilities, but you also need to allow yourself time and activities that replenish your body and mind. If you fail to take care of yourself, you will become so exhausted that your instruction and classroom management will suffer. Give yourself permission to enjoy life so that you will continue to enjoy teaching.

JOURNAL TOPICS

- Describe a teacher whom you consider a professional. What characteristics does he have? What kind of professional activities does he engage in? What makes you view him differently from other teachers?
- Chart your projected growth as a professional. What benchmarks do you envision? What image would you like to project? How do you want your students to view you? How do you want parents to view you? How do you want your colleagues to view you?

References

Bloom, B., Englehart, M., Furst, E., Hill, W., & Krathwohl, D. (1956). *Taxonomy of educational, objectives: Handbook I—Cognitive domain.* New York: David McKay.

Briggs, C., Tully, B., & Stiefer, T. (1998). Direct informed assessment: Frequency of use in preservice teacher education programs within a five-state region. *Action in Teacher Education, 20*(3), 30–39.

Burden, P., & Byrd, D. (1994). *Methods for effective teaching.* Boston: Allyn & Bacon.

Canter, L., & Canter, M. (1976). *Assertive discipline: A take-charge approach for today's educator.* Los Angeles: Canter Associates.

Doll, W. (1993). *A post-modern perspective on curriculum.* New York: Teachers College Press.

Gardner, H. (1993). *Multiple intelligences: The theory in practice.* New York: Basic Books.

Harrow, A. (1972). *Taxonomy of the psychomotor domain: A guide for developing behavior objectives.* New York: David McKay.

Kellough, R. (1999). *Surviving your first year of teaching: Guidelines for success.* Upper Saddle River, NJ: Merrill.

Kilpatrick, W. (1993). *Why Johnny can't tell right from wrong: And what we can do about it.* New York: Touchstone.

Krathwohl, D., Bloom, B., & Masia, B. (1964). *Taxonomy of educational objectives: Handbook II—Affective domain.* New York: David McKay.

Linn, R. (1996). *A teacher's introduction to postmodernism.* Urbana, IL: National Council of Teachers of English.

Macrorie, K. (1980). *Searching writing.* Rochelle Park, NJ: Hayden.

Mager, R. (1984). *Preparing instructional objectives* (2nd ed.). Belmont, CA: David S. Lake.

Marzano, R., & Kendall, J. (2006). *The new taxomony of educational objectives.* Thousand Oaks, CA: Corwin Press.

Moore, K. (1999). *Middle and secondary school instructional methods* (2nd ed.). New York: McGraw-Hill.

Moore, K. (2005). *Effective instructional strategies: From theory to practice.* Thousand Oaks, CA. Sage.

Orlich, D., Harder, R., Callahan, R., & Gibson, H. (2001). *Teaching strategies: A guide to better instruction* (6th ed.). Boston: Houghton Mifflin.

Ornstein, A. (1990). *Strategies for effective teaching.* New York: Harper & Row.

Simpson, M. (2000, November). *Protecting student privacy* [18 paragraphs]. Retrieved October 19, 2006, from www.findarticles.com/p/articles/mi_qa3617/is_2000/ai_n8920562

Smith, M. (2005, January). Howard Gardner and multiple intelligences. *The encyclopedia of informal education.* Retrieved October 19, 2006, from www.infed.org/thinkers/gardner.htm

Tomlinson, C. (2001). *How to differentiate instruction in mixed-ability classrooms* (2nd ed.). Alexandria, VA: Association for Supervision and Curriculum Development.

Tompkins, G. (1998). *Language arts: Content and strategies* (4th ed.). Upper Saddle River, NJ: Merrill.

Wong, H., & Wong, R. (1991). *The first days of school.* Sunnyvale, CA: Harry K. Wong.

Wyatt, R. (1990). A mini-course for journal writers. In C. Goss (Ed.), *Write angles II: More strategies for teaching composition* (pp. 15–24). Oklahoma City: State Department of Education.

Wyatt, R., & Looper, S. (2003). *So you have to have a portfolio: A teacher's guide to preparation and presentation* (2nd ed.). Thousand Oaks, CA: Corwin Press.

CORWIN PRESS

The Corwin Press logo—a raven striding across an open book—represents the union of courage and learning. Corwin Press is committed to improving education for all learners by publishing books and other professional development resources for those serving the field of PreK–12 education. By providing practical, hands-on materials, Corwin Press continues to carry out the promise of its motto: **"Helping Educators Do Their Work Better."**